Bullyproof Your Workplace

Strategies to Prevent Workplace Bullying

Rae A. Stonehouse

Live For Excellence Productions

Copyright

ISBN - E-book: 978-1-998813-23-0

ISBN – Paperback: 978-1-998813-24-7

ISBN – Audiobook: 978-1-998813-25-4

Contents

Introduction

Many of us might recall schoolyard bullies from our school days. Well, guess what? Many bullies have grown-up into not so well-adjusted adults.

Odds are you will experience them in your workplace. If their bullying behavior worked for them in the past, they may continue to do so.

As a recently retired registered nurse of over four decades, having worked predominantly in psychiatry/mental health, I've encountered more than my share of workplace bullies.

This book is divided into two parts. ***Part One: A Personal Perspective*** and ***Part Two: Best Practices to Prevent Bullying in The Workplace.***

Part One is directed to workers currently experiencing bullying in their workplace and provides sage advice on understanding what is happening and what can be done about it.

In Part One I provide examples and situations from my experience working in healthcare. The examples and the lessons learned apply to other worksites.

In Part Two we take a higher-level look at the problem with

bullying in the workplace and provide best practices solutions to prevent it.

While the field of Occupational Health & Safety is improving, you will find many employers don't care, don't know about OH&S matters or who actively ignore regulations for increased profit. OH&S legislation is in place to deal with those employers. Worker's Compensation boards are gaining more authority and clout in many jurisdictions and have been levying hefty fines for employers who don't comply.

After you read Part One, the book isn't written to be read linearly i.e., from front to back. As in my other personal/professional self-development books I use what I call an 'onion' method. I explore a topic in depth and often peel back a layer and revisit a topic from a different perspective. The chapters can be used for future reference.

William Feathers is often quoted as saying "knowledge is power." I disagree with Mr. Feathers and believe knowledge is only power when you do something with it.

This book will give you the knowledge and the power to do something about bullies. Bullies at work, or elsewhere in our lives, are no longer acceptable.

Onwards and upwards!

Rae A. Stonehouse,
    Author
    April 2023

* * *

Part One

Part One: A Personal Perspective

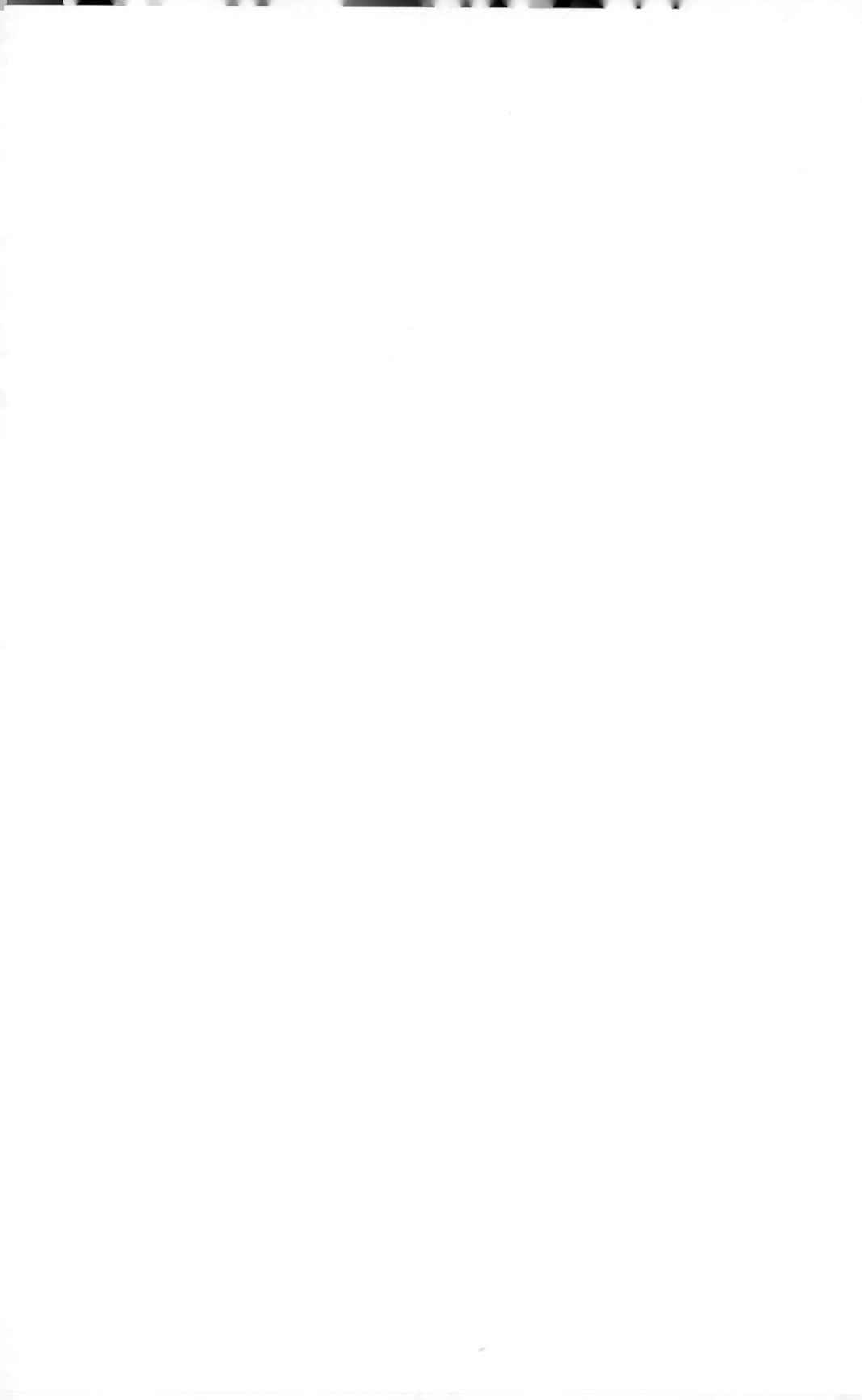

A Personal Perspective

What is bullying? Bullying is persistent unwelcome behavior, mostly using needless or invalid criticism, nitpicking, fault finding, also exclusion, isolation, being singled out and treated differently, being shouted at, humiliated, excessive tracking, having verbal and written warnings imposed, and much more. In the workplace, bullying usually focuses on distorted or fabricated allegations of underperformance.

According to the late Tim Field creator of Bully Online, bullying differs from harassment and discrimination because the focus is rarely based on gender, race, or disability. The focus is often on competence, or rather the alleged lack of competence of the bullied person. In reality, the target of bullying is often competent and popular, and the bully is aggressively projecting their own social, interpersonal and professional inadequacy onto their target. Projection is to avoid facing up to that inadequacy and doing something about it, and to distract and divert attention away from the bully's inadequacies, shortcomings and failings.

Why do people bully? The purpose of bullying is to hide inadequacy. Bullying has nothing to do with managing etc. ... good managers manage, bad managers bully. Management is managing; bullying is not managing. So, anyone who bullies admits their inadequacy, and the extent to which a person bullies is a measure of their inadequacy. Bullies project their inadequacy on to others:

a) to avoid facing up to their inadequacy and doing something about it;

b) to avoid accepting responsibility for their behavior and the effect it has on others,

and mainly,

c) to divert attention away from their inadequacy in an insecure or badly managed workplace, this is how inadequate, incompetent and aggressive employees keep their jobs.

Bullying is an inefficient way of working, resulting in disenchantment, demoralization, demotivation, disaffection, and alienation. Bullies run dysfunctional and inefficient organizations; staff turnover and sickness absence are high, whilst morale, productivity and profitability are low. Prosperity is illusory and such organizations are a bad long-term investment. Projection and denial are hallmarks of the serial bully.

Bullying is present behind all forms of harassment, discrimination, prejudice, abuse, persecution, conflict and violence. When bullying has a focus (e.g., race or gender) it comes out as racial prejudice or harassment, or sexual discrimination and harassment, and so on.

How to Spot a Bullying Employer:

You may be dazzled by corporate visions, mission statements, or by impressive badges on glossy paper, and whilst sometimes these may be deserved, some quality and people awards, can be used by unscrupulous employers to hide what's going on. The best guide to what it's like to work for an employer is to get the following information covering at least the last twelve months. A good employer will be happy to divulge this information. (Apart from stress breakdowns, some employers, especially the larger ones, may have a few for genuine or unrelated reasons):

- rate of staff turnover
- amount of sick leave
- number of stress breakdowns
- number of deaths in service
- number of ill health retirements
- number of early retirements
- number of uses of disciplinary procedures
- number of grievances initiated
- number of suspensions
- number of dismissals
- number of uses of private security firms to snoop on employees
- number of times the employer is involved in industrial tribunals or legal action against employees

People who are bullied find they are:

- constantly criticized
- explanations and proof of achievement are ridiculed, overruled, dismissed or ignored
- forever subject to nit picking and trivial fault finding (the triviality is the giveaway)

- undermined, especially in front of others; false concerns are raised, or doubts are expressed over a person's performance or standard of work however, the doubts lack substantive and quantifiable evidence, for they are only the bully's unreliable opinion
- overruled, ignored, sidelined, marginalized, ostracized
- isolated and excluded from what's happening (this makes people more vulnerable and easier to control and subjugate)
- singled out and treated differently (for example everyone else can have long lunch breaks, but if they are one minute late it's a disciplinary offense)
- belittled, degraded, demeaned, ridiculed, patronized
- threatened, shouted at and humiliated, especially in front of others
- taunted and teased where the intention is to embarrass and humiliate
- set unrealistic goals and deadlines which are unachievable or which are changed without notice or reason or whenever they get near achieving them
- denied information or knowledge for undertaking work and achieving objectives
- denied support by their manager and find themselves working in a management vacuum either overloaded with work (this keeps people busy [with no time to tackle bullying] and makes it harder to achieve targets) or have all their work taken away (which is sometimes replaced with inappropriate menial jobs, e.g., photocopying, filing, making coffee)
- have their responsibility increased but their authority removed
- have their work plagiarized, stolen and copied the bully then presents their target's work (e.g., to senior management) as their own

- are given the silent treatment: the bully refuses to communicate and avoids eye contact; often instructions are received only via email, memos
- subject to excessive tracking, supervision, micro management, recording, snooping, etc.
- the subject of written complaints by other members of staff (most of whom have been coerced into fabricating allegations - the complaints are trivial, often bizarre ["He looked at me in a funny way"] and often bear striking similarity to each other, suggesting a common origin)
- find requests for leave have unacceptable and unnecessary conditions attached, sometimes overturning previous approval, especially if the person has addressed bullying in the meantime
- denied annual leave, sickness leave, or especially compassionate leave
- when on leave, are harassed by calls at home or on holiday, often at unsocial hours
- receive unpleasant or threatening calls or are harassed with intimidating memos, notes or e-mails with no verbal communication, right before weekends and holidays (e.g., 4 pm Friday or Christmas Eve - often these are hand delivered)
- do not have a clear job description, or have one that is exceedingly long or vague; the bully often deliberately makes the person's role unclear
- are invited to "informal" meetings which turn out to be disciplinary hearings
- are denied representation at meetings, often under threat of further disciplinary action; sometimes the bully abuses their position of power to exclude any representative competent to deal with bullying
- encouraged to feel guilty, and to believe they're always the one at fault

- subjected to unwarranted and unjustified verbal or written warnings
- facing unjustified disciplinary action on trivial or specious or false charges
- facing dismissal on fabricated charges or flimsy excuses, often using a trivial incident from months or years previously
- coerced into reluctant resignation, enforced redundancy i.e., layoff, early or ill health retirement

As an Individual, What Can I Do About It?

Bullying is hard to prove, as it takes place behind closed doors with no witnesses and no evidence (in the traditional sense at least). When called to account, the bully uses charm and their Jekyll and Hyde nature to lie convincingly. Bullies are clever, but you can be clever too.

Here's how:

Step 1: Regain Control.

- Recognize what is happening to you as bullying. It is the bully who has the problem which he or she is projecting on to you.
- Criticisms and allegations, which are ostensibly about you or your performance and which sometimes have a grain (but only a grain) of truth, are not about you or your performance. Do not be fooled by that grain of truth into believing the criticisms and allegations have any validity they do not. The purpose of criticism is

control; it has nothing to do with performance enhancement.

- Criticisms and allegations are a projection of the bully's own weaknesses, shortcomings, failings and incompetence; every criticism or allegation is an admission by the bully of their misdeeds and wrongdoing, something they have said or done or did not do.

- You may be encouraged to feel shame, embarrassment, guilt, and fear this is a normal reaction, but misplaced and inappropriate. This is how all abusers, including child sex abusers, control and silence their victims.

- You cannot handle bullying by yourself bullies use deception, amoral behavior and abuse of power. Get help. There is no shame or failure in this the bully is devious, deceptive, evasive and manipulative and cheats. Often, the bully is behaving like a sociopath.

Step 2: Take Action.

- Keep a log (journal, diary) of everything – it's not each incident that counts, it's the number, regularity and especially the pattern that reveal bullying. With most forms of mystery, deception, etc. the patterns are important. The bully can explain individual incidents but cannot explain away the pattern. It's the pattern which reveals intent.

- Keep your diary in a safe place, not at work where others can steal it; keep it at home and keep photocopies of important documents in a separate location (not at work); in several cases the bully has rifled the desk drawers of their target, stolen the diary and then used it as "evidence" of misconduct.

- Keep copies of all letters, memos, e-mails, etc. Get and keep everything in writing otherwise the bully will deny everything later.

- Carry a notepad and pen with you and record everything that the bully says and does. Also note every interaction with staff, management, and anyone else connected with the bullying. Expect to be accused of "misconduct" and a few other things when you do this.

- Record everything in writing; when criticisms or allegations are made, write and ask the bully to substantiate their criticisms and allegations in writing by providing substantive and quantifiable evidence. When the bully doesn't reply or fails to supply substantive and quantifiable evidence, write again pointing out you've asked for justification and the bully has chosen not to reply or has not justified their claim. On the third occasion point out, in writing, that making allegations and refusing to substantiate them in writing or failing to provide substantive and quantifiable evidence is a form of harassment. The bully's criticisms and allegations, which are usually founded on distortion, blame and fabrication, are an opinion or fabrication for control.

- Denial is everywhere. The person who asserts their right not to be bullied is often blowing the whistle on another's incompetence (which the bullying is intended to hide). Expect the bully to deny everything, expect the bully's superiors to deny and disbelieve everything, expect staff /human resources to disbelieve you and deny the bullying, for they will already have been deceived by the bully into joining in with the bully and getting rid of you.

- The serial bully likes to play people off against each other so try to reunite yourself with your employer against the bully. Point out firmly but politely to your Human Resources (HR) people that the serial bully is encouraging the employer and employee and to engage in destructive conflict in which there are no winners, only losers. The bully gains gratification from manipulating and watching others destroy each other. If the bully realizes they've been rumbled they will move on leaving the employer to incur all the vicarious liability for their behavior. The bully has done this before and will do it again.

- Build yourself a support network. Bullies separate and isolate their targets, sometimes causing division within the target's family. The bully will likely manipulate your work colleagues into distancing themselves from you, either by sweet talking them with charm, or by playing on their vulnerabilities whilst raising doubts about their job security.

- See your doctor bullying causes prolonged negative stress which causes psychiatric injury.

- Psychiatric injury has nothing to do with mental illness, despite what others (including some mental health professionals) may say or infer. If stress is diagnosed, make sure it includes the cause, e.g., stress caused by conditions in the workplace. If depression is diagnosed, make sure it is recorded as reactive depression. Remember that stress is not the employee's inability to cope with excessive workload but a result of the employer's failure to provide a safe system of work.

- Take the matter up with your line management beware though, most bullies are the line manager and are supported by their line manager, etc. Often, the bullying is hierarchical and comes from the top.

- Obtain a copy of your employer's bullying and harassment policy. You might wish to do this discreetly (e.g., through a third party) if you're not yet ready to challenge the bully.

- Contact occupational health bullying causes prolonged negative stress which causes injury to health and if it continues may culminate in psychiatric injury.

- You are unlikely to be the only person to contact your OH&S department and you may not be the first to name the bully.

- Reassure and educate your partner/family that your symptoms are a psychiatric injury and will improve. Encourage those around you to read up on bullying and PTSD (Post-Traumatic Stress Disorder).

- Inform your employer that your psychiatric injury (and the ill health of others) is due to bullying by another member of staff and that this employee's behavior is a danger to the health & safety of employees; highlight the high staff turnover in that individual's department and the corresponding amount of sickness absence / stress breakdowns / early and ill health retirement / attempted or actual suicides / deaths in service.

- Follow the grievance procedure but beware that such procedures may be biased for the manager, as well as being inappropriate for dealing with bullying.

- Understand the profile of the serial bully and emphasize the Jekyll and Hyde nature and compulsive lying. The bully will already have deceived staff and his/her superiors. If you go to an employment tribunal later, the tribunal will look to see if you've followed all the options open to you (even if they work or not).

- If the bully prevents you from being accompanied to grievance and disciplinary meetings, check your rights under your country's law.

- If the bully is making needless criticisms in public or on your record, you may feel it appropriate to ask your solicitor to write a letter to the bully pointing out that he or she is subject to the laws of slander, libel, and defamation of character.

- If your employer refuses to get involved, or backs the bully in his/her attempt to get rid of you, you might ask your solicitor to write to someone in authority (with legal responsibility) outlining the way your manager has treated you, stating that your rights in law will be vigorously defended against the unacceptable behavior of one of their employees whose actions will be tracked due to his or her declared intentions. This turns the spotlight on the bully rather than on the target. If your employer is unwilling to address the bullying perhaps because the bullying is hiding incompetence endemic in the organization expect fireworks.

- Consider leaving. Regard it as a positive decision in the face of overwhelming odds not of your choosing, not of your making, and over which you have no control. Serial bullies are obsessive and compulsive in their behavior; once they start on their target, they won't let go until that person is destroyed.

- For most people, the top priority is to be financially stable. What's more important job or health? You may need to move on and find an employer who values you and your skills. Refuse to let your health be destroyed and your career wrecked by an idiot.

- If you are forced into leaving, make it clear to your employer in writing this is due to bullying. Get professional advice before signing anything.

- Do your utmost to obtain an agreed reference. Without one you may not get another job, especially in the professions. Most employers require a reference from your previous employer and the bully never misses the opportunity to sabotage your career.

- The Number One mistake people make is to not recognize the serial bully as a sociopath. Naivety is the greatest enemy most people can't or won't believe that the person their tackling is a sociopath and expect the bully to recognize their wrongdoing and make amends. Sociopaths cannot and will not, but they will ruthlessly exploit other people's naivety to ensure their own survival. Never underestimate the serial bully's deviousness, ruthlessness, cunning, and ability to deceive.

Phrases you might find useful:

"By the way s/he chooses to behave, s/he prevents myself and others from fulfilling our duties."

. . .

"By the way s/he chooses to behave, s/he brings her/himself, the staff, the department and the employer into disrepute."

"The purpose of bullying is to hide inadequacy; bullying is a breach of the implied term of mutual trust and confidence."

"Your criticisms and allegations lack substantive and quantifiable evidence."

If you are fighting a case of bullying against a serial bully and the employer chooses to not respond positively, remember the Achilles heels:

- Bullying is an obsessive-compulsive behavior and repetitive; it's often a lifetime behavior. It is most likely the serial bully has a history of this behavior which a little investigation will reveal.

- The serial bully displays arrogance and expects to get away with their behavior.
- Serial bullying is highly predictable.
- The serial bully is usually a compulsive liar with a Jekyll and Hyde nature therefore their words cannot be trusted. Highlight this at every opportunity.

- When dealing with the serial bully, concentrate on the patterns of incidents rather than the incidents themselves (which are often trivial when taken out of context). The bully can always explain individual incidents, but s/he cannot explain the pattern. When discussing any single incident, refer repeatedly to the pattern of which this incident is part.

- Bullies are adept at creating conflict between those who would otherwise pool negative information; make it clear to your employer that the bully is working his or her own self-interest and gains gratification from encouraging the employer and employee to engage in destructive conflict. Remind your employer that the bully is deliberately and willfully causing the employer to incur vicarious liability for their behavior.

- The purpose of bullying is to hide inadequacy, and people who bully to hide their inadequacy are often incompetent, the worse the bullying, the greater and more widespread the incompetence. Abusive employers will often pay large out of court settlements to keep that incompetence secret.

- If all else fails, and legal action proves impossible, remember Klingon wisdom: bortaS bIr jablu'DI'reH QaQqu' nay' which translates as Revenge is a dish best served cold: give media interviews, write articles, contribute to research, or write a book ... use those qualities of competence, popularity, integrity and courage of which the bully was jealous.

The above discussion on Bullying was adapted from information posted on Bully Online circa 1996. Tim Field, the owner of the site, had granted permission to distribute and use the material. Sadly, Tim has passed on.

Something to remember about what we have just read is that it refers to a person with some form of power over you i.e., a boss or supervisor. It could be a coworker who is the bully or at least displays bully-like behavior. Remember, that one cause identified for bullying is an inadequate personality. A coworker could easily target you if they are the bullying type and use that behavior in the workplace.

Intervention Process for Bullying:

☐ Review Incident
    ☐ Gain Control
    ☐ Find Help
    ☐ Plan for Action
    ☐ Document
    ☐ Confront
    ☐ Formal Written Complaint
    ☐ Legal Action

Incident Review:

• • •

• **Gain Control:** Recognize that the aggressor is at fault --- not you. Take the time you need to acknowledge the impact of the incident and the emotions it triggers for you. Consider acting immediately during the incident or soon after. Know that only 25% of targets and witnesses feel able to confront the bully during the incident, 75% do not. Confronting may involve disengaging from the bully.

• **Find Help from your union if you are a member of one, colleagues and your employer:** Read your workplace policy on harassment or violence to understand your options.

• **Make an Action Plan.** Gather the support you feel you need, rather than proceeding alone. Seek advice from others with similar experiences, talk to your union steward (if you have one), your manager (assuming they are not the bully!) or counselor, and take advantage of employee assistance programs.

• **Document:** Use the 4Ws --- who, what, when & where and explain the context of the situation. Keep a detailed log of all incidents with names of witnesses. If your health is affected by these events, see your healthcare provider.

• **Confront the aggressor.** Make it clear that the behavior is offensive and must stop. Speak from the first-person viewpoint using the word "I" and describe the specific behavior and how it made you feel. You need not do this alone, gather any support you feel you need before, during and after the intervention.

• • •

•**Make a formal written complaint.** Follow the employer's respectful workplace complaint policy (if they have one)

•**Take Legal Action.** It may be appropriate if the situation remains unresolved to consider seeking expert legal advice.

Our explanation of bullying has been generalized to cover all vocations or work environments. It exists in healthcare. I would expect that we have all experienced it in our careers but perhaps weren't aware of what was happening to us. Or conversely, if we were aware, we felt powerless to do anything about it.

Field, having been bullied himself at work, puts it into perspective and calls it for what it is ... workplace violence. He outlines methods of recognizing a workplace bully and strategies to neutralize them. His books are a must read for anyone currently experiencing bullying behavior or advocates on behalf of others.

I would like to share with you a personal story of my experience with a serial bully in the workplace. It has provided me with the impetus to finish and publish this book that you are reading. It has been over three decades since the incident. It can take a while to recover from the symptoms of PTSD. Some don't. I was one of the lucky ones.

In 1999 I was writing a book with the focus on violence in the workplace. I had included a section on bullying but was blind-sided when I became a victim myself.

. . .

To set the scene, I was an active participant in an online web forum entitled Nurse Advocate. Its mandate was to raise awareness and provide resources to reduce workplace violence. I regularly provided feedback and/or suggestions to support people, healthcare providers, that had experienced violence in the workplace. Common themes of discussion were the isolation the person felt, the lack of support from their fellow staff or their managers, the insinuation that they had brought the violence on to themselves and the range of negative emotions that resulted.

I was working in a psychiatric unit in a small community as a staff nurse in a casual capacity. Casual, meaning I was on call for all my shifts. After three years of casual, I succeeded in obtaining a full-time, although temporary position to replace another nurse off on extended sick leave. Three days into this new position, things changed rapidly.

I was well aware I was working in a dysfunctional workplace. There were staff who wouldn't work with others due to a disagreement ten years earlier. Some would change their schedule so as not to have to work with certain individuals. The dysfunction started at the top with the manager and trickled downward. There was a sense of oppression evident where the staff were afraid to voice their opinions in a public forum. The manager was overt in her attempt to split staff, one against the other. She also had her group of confidants that kept her informed of events. She was reported to have gone through staff wastepaper baskets after work hours looking for evidence to use against individual staff.

In a united front, the ward staff organized an off-duty meeting with union stewards in attendance to develop initiatives to deal with this bullying manager. Different initiatives were forwarded. Some ideas were a little more militant than others. I am a logical, pragmatic thinker and offered those suggestions were inappropriate. I tried to provide some levity to the situation by making a joke. "We are not dealing with a logical person here. The only logical thing is to pass a hat, take a collection and put a hit on her." Yes, dear reader, I can hear you cringing. I would do anything as the saying goes to take that utterance back. Life doesn't work that way though. After a few laughs, it went unnoticed... until the next day.

I received a summons to go to a disciplinary hearing to account for my issuing death threats. I was in a state of shock and wasn't aware of what they were talking about. Fortunately, one benefit of being in the temporary position was that I was a member of our local union which provided me representation. I brought my steward with me to my surprise disciplinary meeting.

At this meeting I learned that one of my fellow nurses, a confidant of the leader being discussed, had recorded the meeting. She had contacted the manager that evening and advised them that there was an assassination plot to wipe out all senior management and that Rae's wife was a trained marksman and would carry out the hit. As incredulous as it seems, I was presented with this information. My wife, also a nurse, has never touched a firearm and abhors hunting animals of any sort.

During the hearing, I apologized profusely for making a "black humor" joke that was taken the wrong way and was sorry for any problems it had caused. This fueled the bully's righteous indignation, and I was terminated on the spot. My union immediately intervened and filed a wrongful dismissal grievance.

· · ·

After returning home, I contacted the RCMP (Royal Canadian Mounted Police) to discover if there was a bench warrant out for my arrest. This is a common practice to deal with situations such as this from a Human Resources perspective. I spoke with the investigating officer who thanked me for contacting him. He advised me "I was called into do an investigation at your workplace as I was asked to do. I advised your managers that it was a joke taken the wrong way, for the wrong reasons. Son, you work in a dysfunctional place. If I were you, I would get out of there as soon as you can."

Thanks to the efforts of my union, within two weeks, I was working in a facility a few blocks away from the original setting, with the same clientele. I was in a different job, and it took three grievances and a year for the process to resolve itself.

I'm sure you can appreciate the stress and anxiety this created for me and my family. It was compounded by information I was hearing from my former work colleagues of how others had said they were affected by this event. It is interesting to see how people can turn against you when it serves their purpose.

A year later, this situation was resolved with a win/win outcome. I secured a new job in a better environment. I received a cash payout to rectify my losses and they got an experienced nurse at the new setting. I had an "invisible" notation on my personnel file that should I utter the same suggestion again, the notation would become "visible." This was to be on file for 18 months. That is an example of how a bully can save face.

. . .

What about the bullying manager? In an interesting twist of the story, a year later, a meeting of some 65 professionals met to discuss how she had affected each of them negatively. Doctors, social workers, nurses, psychologists... all shared their stories of how she had hurt them personally.

Three unions went to the CEO of the organization, and she was immediately "unhired". She wasn't actually terminated. It allowed senior management save face. An era had come to an end. But was she ever held accountable? We don't know. Since then, she has had problems keeping jobs. A bullying manager is not acceptable.

I don't want to leave you with the idea that I was an innocent victim in this situation. I was stupid in several ways and I take full responsibility for my actions. I was stupid because I underestimated the lengths a bully will go to maintain control. I was stupid because I provided the bully ammo, so to speak, to act against me to remove me as a threat.

It had occurred to me sometime after the event that I had gone on public record shortly before my termination in opposing an initiative that she was promoting. I was also stupid for saying what I did, even though it was meant as a joke. I later heard in a conversation that the manager had actually targeted me two years earlier and had made the comment publicly that she would get me sooner or later. Bullies will always get even.

So, what did I learn in this situation?

. . .

I learned first-hand the effects of post-traumatic stress disorder (PTSD). I experienced intrusive thoughts for close to a year. Thinking about the manager would cause me to be distressed. I had many sleepless nights. It caused me to be hypervigilant in performing my job. What was coming next? It caused me to mistrust my former coworkers and my new ones. I became reluctant to talk to anyone as you never know if what you say will come back to haunt you as when taken out of context.

I know of fellow workers that if you mentioned this manager's name, they would start to display PTSD symptoms. That is the effect that a bully can have on you if you let them.

There was a turning point for me though. As we were approaching the one-year anniversary and an arbitration hearing to finally resolve this matter, I realized that they could take my job away from me, but they couldn't take my dignity. I had lots of other options available should I lose my nursing license. That isn't what a bully wants. They want you to lose hope. They want to take your dignity. That is how they maintain control and feel good about themselves. This realization strengthened me and let me be an active participant in the resolution process.

I also found the whole situation to be embarrassing. Working in healthcare for so many years, I don't get embarrassed easily, but this situation did. Here I was writing a book on workplace violence, having done significant research on the subject and I go and commit it myself. It just shows me how insidious workplace violence is. We aren't always aware of its presence. And we aren't aware of how our actions can be used against us. As the police officer said... "by the wrong people, for the wrong reasons."

. . .

Since then, I have made it my mission in life to challenge anyone using a similar type of dark humor. It is inappropriate and dangerous. You don't know how it will be interpreted. I have shared my story with many people in the hope they won't have to experience what I did.

As I sit here at the keyboard writing this chapter, I'm finding it interesting, if not somewhat depressing, reflecting on the number of other incidents throughout my life where I have come up against bullies. There always seems another around the corner!

As a child I was easily intimidated. At six years of age a bully at my bus stop threw my pet cat under the wheels of the school bus. She had followed me several times before to the stop and then returned home on her own after I had left in the bus. In the days following, I viewed the blood stain of my pet on the pavement as I awaited my bus. Sixty years later, I still remember the incident vividly. The following year, at a different school, I was forced into paying protection money to a "tomboy" of a girl, so she wouldn't beat me up. In an odd twist of fate, I understand that she eventually became a kindergarten teacher. Those poor children!

Children that are bullies often become bullies as adults. My father was a bully and used intimidation and force to rule his family. I have no way of knowing if he was a bully when he was young, but I know for a fact that his mother, my grandmother, was. I was hit regularly whenever one of my siblings got into trouble. "You're the oldest. It's your job to keep them out of trouble!" I remember him being an angry man.

. . .

Using the adage of "if the only tool in your toolbox is a hammer, then every problem is a nail", then we as children were his nails.

One observation I have had about some bullies is that when you confront them on their behavior, they can be surprised that they are seen that way by others. Then their feelings are hurt, and they take it personally. I haven't found mention of it in my review of the literature, but I believe there is a class of bully I would call the "situational bully."

The situational bully is displaying many of the bully-like behaviors consistent to what we have read above but their motive is different. At a conscious level I don't know if they are aware of how they are relating to others, or perhaps it is a conditioned response.

We all respond differently to different personality types, often based on our experiences with similar types of personalities. We often repeat our ways of interacting with types of people who we have had problems with, in similar ways with others that bear a resemblance, at least in our minds, to those original ones.

This is dysfunctional. Bullying is still bullying, and it isn't acceptable. The point I want to make here is that while it is usually easy to recognize bullying in other people and if you are being bullied, you will know. However, will you recognize it in yourself? It is easy to fall into a pattern of bullying if you are in a situation, you don't have the skills to effectively handle it.

This section is intended to raise your awareness and leave you with a sense of hope. We need not put up with bullies anymore.

. . .

Note: My personal comments throughout this section reflect a 40-year nursing career. As of January 2020, I retired from nursing.

I worked another 20 years in the position and the location I was awarded as part of my grievance settlement. It had a happy ending with me becoming a valued employee and nurse, however, it was a tortuous journey to get to that point.

I took several years to recover from the bullying incident. I became a union steward myself to ensure others wouldn't go through the same struggles I did. I became an anti-bullying advocate and challenged bullying in my workplace.

I developed influence within the facility by taking a leadership role in our Occupational Health & Safety program as well as becoming a mentor for my support staff.

After retirement, I had considered going back to work on a casual basis, however, Covid-19 prevented me from doing so.

As I reflect on 40 years of nursing, I'm aware I was fear-based throughout my career. I've encountered many bullies over the years, almost all were in leadership positions.

My wife, also a nurse shares a similar philosophy and that is "waiting for the other shoe to drop."

As nurses we held an inordinate amount of responsibility. Our organizations tended to play the blame game. I'm happy to say these organizations eventually bought into the idea of being learning organizations.

As learning organizations, they looked at causes and effects of incidents strategically, rather than the age-old reaction to finding blame and punishing someone.

* * *

Calley provides an enlightening story of the pressures she experienced in starting to work in a dysfunctional workplace. Names have been changed to protect the guilty.

Imagine how it would be to finally find meaningful employment as a Care Aide after a long and tedious job search only to find that your new worksite is toxic. And the toxicity was aimed at you... the newcomer. Or so it seems, from your perspective.

From the first days of her orientation to the new job, Calley noticed her fellow staff weren't all that friendly toward her. It wasn't obvious at first, but Calley could sense they were treating her differently.

Conversations would stop when she walked into the office. When her coworkers were going for a "coffee run" she wouldn't be asked if she was interested. Her contributions in shift report or staff meetings were dismissed by certain staff. "When you've been here long enough, you'll see things differently." "What do you know, you're new here!"

. . .

Yet everybody else seemed to get along fine.

There always seemed to be a party at somebody's home. Calley wasn't invited. Some of her coworkers would switch their shifts so they could work with each other or to work with a certain nurse when they were in charge. Calley found she seemed to take most of her coffee breaks alone. Her fellow staff would have other matters to tend to when their coffee break was due.

Calley relates "I expected some challenges when starting a new job... being the new kid on the block, but this seemed over the top."

Several months into working at her new job, Calley sensed that some residents seemed to act differently when nurse Flo was on shift. Some seemed more sedated than would be expected. Others seemed timid or perhaps fearful in the presence of Flo. When Flo was on duty, many residents received sedation. Flo liked the unit to be calm. It didn't matter what time of day it was; Flo liked her residents to be quiet.

On several occasions Calley had seen Flo shouting and berating residents for their behavior. Calley related that she felt intimidated by Flo so didn't confront her directly but mentioned her observations to a few of her fellow care-aides. She was met with hostility and shunning. The "old" staff seemed to protect this nurse and condone the behavior.

Calley reported her concerns to the Team Leader who dismissed those concerns. They spoke supporting Flo. At about this time Calley was spending a considerable amount of her off-duty time thinking about her working conditions. She found her sleep was restless at times with intrusive dreams of work. Perhaps it was time to look for another job?

On a couple of occasions Calley observed Flo shouting at residents from the medication room, down the hall, to come and get their medications. This seemed acceptable to her fellow staff and nobody seemed concerned when she voiced her opinion that this wasn't a respectful way to treat residents.

The final straw, so to speak, came one day when Calley observed Flo shaking a resident. The resident was watching TV and Flo approached the resident grabbing them by both shoulders and shaking. "When I tell you that medications are ready, I expect you to get your ass over there and get them! Do you hear me? Are you deaf? You better do as you are told, or you will be sorry!"

Calley shared this story with her fellow care-aides and found no support. She reported it to her Team Leader and experienced a similar response. It was only when the residents themselves approached the Team Leader to complain, was action taken. The local Licensing Department was contacted, and Flo was suspended pending investigation.

Was this the end of the story? Not according to Calley... it was only the beginning! Flo started a phone campaign to smear Calley and make life miserable for her. Each of the staff were phoned and advised that "Calley was a rat." "Don't turn your back on her, she will stab you!"

. . .

This flowed back to the worksite where her fellow staff who had been avoidant and dismissive of her now became openly hostile. Flo took on the victim role and created a story where she was the wrongfully treated hero of the saga. Guess who was the bad guy?

Calley's time at work became absolute misery. Fellow staff would call her "Bitch" to her face and behind her back. Similar sentiments were scrawled on pieces of paper and stuck to the front of her locker. One nurse was openly hostile toward her. "Bitch. I hope you're happy, you've ruined the life of a good nurse. You don't deserve to work here. No wonder nobody likes you!" This was repeated several days in a row when Calley was scheduled to work with this nurse. Calley was losing sleep at night and started to phone in sick when she had to work with these staff.

As part of the investigation Calley was asked to document her observations of the abusive nurse, which she did reluctantly. No other staff submitted support for her. It was Calley's word against the nurse's. The resident's testimony was not given much weight.

Flo was eventually returned to duty with a sanction on her personnel record. She maximized her victim role and relished the power that it gave her in the worksite. Calley left the worksite because of the continuing pressure. She eventually returned after a couple years. Many of the staff who had worked there at the time had moved on, but not Flo. She continued to make sure that every staff that worked there was aware that "Calley was a rat!" Every interaction she had with Calley from then on, was openly hostile.

. . .

If you asked Calley today whether she would do it again, she would respond "No way! It was absolute Hell what they put me through. Nobody should be treated that way."

Flo's behavior eventually caught up with her and incompetence in nursing practice led to a fellow nurse taking actions with the nursing licensing board. Flo was suspended from practice and retired.

Analysis:

If we look closely at this story, what can we take away or learn from Calley's experiences?

Starting off with Assessment, what do we know about this worksite?

- There seems to be an "old boys" network in place or a clique. Newcomers were not welcomed into it.
- There was a shroud of silence where workers didn't talk or even acknowledge the untoward actions of others.
- Interpersonal hostility toward new staff was the norm rather than the exception.
- Certain staff had more "power" over others than what was part of their job description.
- The residents were not treated respectfully.
- The Team Leader and presumably administration condoned dysfunctional behavior by one of its nurses or at least ignored dealing with it.
- Reporting inappropriate actions by fellow staff resulted in you being labeled as a rat.

- Passive aggressive behavior was rampant, e.g., open messages left on lockers.
- Aggressive behavior was tolerated.
- Lack of cohesiveness and inclusiveness with new and existing staff i.e., us vs. them mentality, with the "us" being the existing staff.

Moving on to Awareness, it would seem obvious to most of us that this was a dysfunctional worksite. More pointedly, there is strong evidence of interpersonal aggression, hostility, bullying and intimidation. This is workplace violence in action. Even sadder, this isn't likely an isolated case.

Our Action phase becomes a little more challenging. What would you do in this situation?

Calley persevered until it got worse. She resolved one part of her working conditions, which made it even worse. She eventually left the worksite. Economic necessity required her to return.

I will remind you that this is a practical guide to preventing and surviving bullying in the workplace. Perhaps the most practical action that Calley could've taken was to quit this job shortly after she learned what the working conditions were like.

The essence of this story is power and control. As the new hire, Calley had neither. Was Flo a bully? Most definitely! Were there other bullies at the worksite? The story doesn't specify so, however bully-like behavior from her fellow staff seemed to be the norm rather than the exception.

When taking on a bully, your self-confidence can be a factor that determines the outcome. If you experience low self-esteem, low self-confidence, the bully will use it against you. However, as this book is all about, knowledge is power, if you use it wisely.

If you have made the decision to stay and take on the bully and the dysfunctional worksite, here are practical steps that you could take to do so. Add your own at any point.

- Flo had an inordinate amount of power in the workplace, at least when she was on shift. Openly challenging her with other staff present would only fuel her attempts to maintain the upper hand. What about the other nurses and care aides? Did they all back and support Flo or were there some that went along with her but didn't condone her behavior? When taking on a bully it is important to ally with your fellow workers. They may not have the courage to stand up on their own.

- Documentation is the key to success when reporting an incident to your manager. It is nearly impossible for your manager to investigate when provided with anecdotal information. It is too easy for the bully to counter accuse or deny, saying that the events never happened or that your interpretation is biased. Collect objective facts. What did you see? Who was involved? Will those involved back up your story? When did the situation take place? Do not flavor your report with an opinion or add your interpretation of why the bully did what they did.

- Familiarize yourself with the tactics that a bully will probably take when accused of wrongdoing. There is great value in predicting a bully's actions.

- If your worksite has a JOSH Committee (Joint Occupational Health & Safety), get the subject of working conditions placed on the agenda. It wouldn't be a good idea to address the bully by name, but there would be value in creating discussion on healthy and respectful workplaces.

Part One Summary:

This section has covered a lot of content and has likely stirred up some memories for you as you have read it, as it has for me to write it. I believe that it is important to remember that many memories of traumatic incidents we had in our childhood were retained or filed away in our vast computer of a brain with the state of development and/or the maturity, intelligence and the skills that we had at the time of the incident. We can't change the past, but we can learn from it.

The past has no power over us. A bully shouldn't wield that control over our life either. Bullies, unfortunately, like the common cold, the flu and other common illnesses, are out there. If you haven't encountered one yet, you are fortunate. You will in time.

. . .

In this section we identified what bullying is and why some people bully. We explored how to spot an employer that bullies. We learned how to regain control of our lives and the decisions that we make. We also learned practical steps we can use to take the power away from a bully, and we looked at a couple case scenarios that illustrated what we have learned.

In the next part we explore bullying in the workplace on a larger scale and introduce organizational preventive strategies.

Rae A. Stonehouse
    Author
    April 2023

* * *

Part Two

Part Two: Best Practices to Prevent Bullying in the Workplace

Introduction: Workplace Bullying And Its Impact On OH&S

Workplace Bullying & Its Forms Defined:

Workplace bullying is the repeated and persistent negative behavior toward an employee or group of employees. It can take various forms, including:

- **Verbal bullying:** This includes name-calling, belittling, sarcasm, and any other form of verbal abuse.
- **Physical bullying:** This involves physical intimidation, such as damaging personal property or physical assault.
- **Psychological bullying:** This type of bullying causes emotional and mental harm, such as spreading rumors, exclusion, or humiliation.
- **Cyberbullying:** This involves the use of technology to bully an employee, such as using social media to spread lies or damaging information.

- **Sexual harassment:** This includes unwanted touching, inappropriate comments, or actions intended to create a sexually hostile work environment.
- **Discrimination:** This involves any action that treats an employee unfairly based on their race, gender, sexual orientation, religion, or disability.

Workplace bullying can have severe implications on an employee's physical and mental health, job satisfaction, and productivity. Employers are responsible for creating a safe workplace environment and must take corrective action if bullying occurs.

The Prevalence of Workplace Bullying and Its Impact on Occupational Health & Safety:

- Workplace bullying is a common problem that affects many employees in various industries and sectors.
- It can take many forms, including verbal abuse, sabotage, exclusion, and intimidation, and can be perpetuated by colleagues, supervisors, or even customers.
- The impact of workplace bullying on occupational health and safety can be severe and long-lasting, including psychological distress, physical symptoms, and increased risk of work-related injury and illness.
- Organizations that do not address workplace bullying risk decreased productivity, increased absenteeism and turnover, and potential legal liability.
- Prevention and intervention strategies should be started at all levels of the organization, including policies and procedures, training and education, and management accountability.

- Employee support services, such as counseling and mediation, are important resources for individuals who have experienced workplace bullying.
- Finally, increasing awareness and understanding of workplace bullying can help to create a safe and supportive workplace culture where all employees feel valued and respected.

Workplace bullying is a pervasive issue that affects millions of workers worldwide, regardless of gender, age, or occupation. According to recent statistics, over 40% of employees in the United States have experienced some form of workplace bullying, while 20% admitted to being a victim of workplace harassment. Workplace bullying can take many forms, including verbal abuse, social exclusion, physical violence, intimidation, and sabotage, among others.

The impact of workplace bullying on occupational health and safety is significant. It can cause severe physical and mental health problems, including stress, anxiety, depression, post-traumatic stress disorder (PTSD), and suicidal thoughts. Victims of workplace bullying are more likely to suffer from chronic health issues such as heart disease, obesity, and diabetes.

Workplace bullying affects not only the victim but also other employees at the workplace. They may feel powerless to intervene or speak up fearing retaliation, resulting in decreased morale and job satisfaction, and increased absenteeism.

Bullying can also have a negative impact on job performance and productivity. Victims may be hesitant to participate in team projects or avoid taking on new responsibilities, which can harm the overall success of the organization. Additionally, those who see bullying may feel less motivated to work hard and may ultimately result in reduced productivity.

Besides the physical and emotional harm inflicted on individuals, there are legal and financial consequences associated with workplace bullying. Employers can be held liable for failing to prevent or address workplace bullying, resulting in costly lawsuits, damage to reputation, and lost profits.

To address this issue, employers need to put comprehensive policies and training into practice programs to prevent and respond to workplace bullying. This includes creating a safe and supportive workplace culture, providing employees with the resources they need to report bullying, and offering support and counseling services to those who have suffered abuse.

Workplace bullying is a serious issue with a significant impact on occupational health and safety, both for the individual and the organization. Employers must try to prevent and address workplace bullying to create a safe and productive work environment for everyone.

* * *

Understanding Different Types
Of Workplace Bullying

Workplace bullying is a serious issue that can be harmful to an individual's physical and emotional well-being, often leading to stress, anxiety, and depression. It can happen in many forms, and identifying the different types of bullying is an essential step in dealing with the issue effectively.

Verbal Bullying:

Verbal bullying is the use of spoken or written language to intimidate, belittle, or humiliate a colleague. It can be shouting, sarcasm, teasing, or gossiping. This type of bullying can be challenging to identify, as it can often be disguised as banter or a joke.

Physical Bullying:

Physical bullying is any form of physical abuse or assault, including pushing, shoving, hitting, or throwing objects. This bullying is often easier to identify, and it can be more harmful to the victim's physical well-being.

Cyberbullying:

Cyberbullying is the use of electronic technology to harass or humiliate a colleague. This can include spreading rumors, insulting messages or social media posts, or unauthorized access to someone's online accounts. Cyberbullying can be challenging to trace, and it can have a severe impact on an individual's emotional well-being.

Sexual Harassment:

Sexual harassment is any form of unwanted sexual attention or behavior, including unwelcome comments, gestures, or physical contact. This bullying is not limited to a particular gender and can have severe consequences, including anxiety, depression, and PTSD.

Indirect Bullying:

Indirect bullying includes behavior meant to hurt or harm another person, but it is not necessarily direct. This may include exclusion from social events, withholding information, or spreading rumors.

Understanding the different types of workplace bullying is crucial in enabling workplaces to identify and prevent it. Employers must be aware of the different types of bullying and take appropriate steps to address and prevent it. By doing this, they can make sure employees are provided with a safe and healthy work environment where they can thrive.

* * *

Recognizing Signs And Symptoms Of Workplace Bullying

Identifying Different Forms of Workplace Bullying:

L earn to recognize signs and symptoms of workplace bullying, including changes in behavior, physical symptoms, and emotional distress.

Workplace bullying is a serious issue that can have a significant impact on the mental and physical health of employees. Workplace bullying takes many forms, including:

Verbal bullying: This is the most common form of workplace bullying. It involves insulting, verbally abusing, shouting at or humiliating an employee. It may also involve constantly criticizing their work or spreading rumors about them.

Physical bullying: This involves physical acts of aggression or violence against an employee. It may include physical threats, pushing, shoving or even assault.

. . .

Social bullying: This type of bullying is more subtle and can involve exclusion, isolation or social manipulation. It often takes the form of spreading rumors or gossip, withholding information, or undermining the social standing of an employee.

Cyberbullying: This form of bullying is becoming more common in the workplace. It includes using technology and social media to harass, bully, or intimidate an employee.

Employers have a responsibility to provide a safe and healthy work environment, including preventing and addressing workplace bullying. If you are experiencing workplace bullying, it is important to speak up and seek help.

How To Identify Workplace Bullying:

As a common issue in the modern-day workplace, bullying can have far-reaching negative effects on the mental and physical well-being of employees. It is crucial to recognize the different types of bullying and their associated signs and symptoms, to address the issue and promote a safe and healthy work environment.

Workplace bullying can take many forms and can range from subtle actions to outright aggression. It is important to be able to identify the signs and symptoms of bullying behavior to address the issue and ensure a safe and respectful workplace.

Some common indicators of workplace bullying include:

Verbal abuse: This includes shouting, name-calling, and belittling comments directed at an individual in the workplace. It can also involve constant criticism of their work or spreading rumors about them.

Intimidation: Intimidation can take many forms, such as physically standing too close to someone, invading personal space, or making threats.

Exclusion: If an individual is often excluded from meetings, activities, or discussions without explanation, this can be a sign of bullying.

Undermining: This can involve making negative comments about an individual's work or abilities, or deliberately sabotaging their efforts.

Overwork: Bullying can also take the form of excessive workload or assigning tasks impossible to complete within a reasonable timeframe.

Isolation: An individual who is constantly isolated or deliberately left out of social interactions or team activities may experience bullying.

Physical abuse: This type of bullying includes physical acts of aggression or violence toward an employee. It may involve physical threats, pushing, shoving, or even assault.

· · ·

Social Bullying: A more subtle form of bullying, social bullying can involve exclusion, isolation, or social manipulation. It often takes the form of spreading rumors or gossip, withholding information, or undermining the social standing of an employee.

Cyberbullying: This type of bullying is becoming more common in the workplace, involving the use of technology and social media to harass, bully, or intimidate an employee.

Employers hold the responsibility of providing a safe and healthy work environment, including preventing and addressing workplace bullying. If you are experiencing any form of workplace bullying, it is essential to speak up and seek help.

If you are experiencing any of these behaviors or symptoms, it is important to speak to your HR department or supervisor. It is also important to document any incidents of workplace bullying, as this can help build a case for addressing the issue. Remember: no one deserves to be bullied, and everyone deserves to work in a safe and respectful workplace.

Here Are Some Indicators of Workplace Bullying to Look Out For:

Verbal Abuse: This may include shouting, name-calling, and belittling comments directed at an individual in the workplace.

Intimidation: Physical intimidation, such as standing too close or making threats, can be a form of bullying.

. . .

Exclusion: Being often excluded from meetings, activities, or discussions without explanation can be a sign of bullying.

Undermining: Negative comments about an individual's work or abilities, or sabotaging their efforts, are examples of undermining.

Overwork: Excessive workload or tasks impossible to complete within a reasonable timeframe can be a form of bullying.

Isolation: Consistent isolation or being deliberately left out of social interactions or team activities may be an indicator of bullying.

Physical Abuse: Acts of aggression or violence, including assault, are physical abuse.

* * *

The Psychological Effects Of Workplace Bullying On The Victims

The Impacts of Workplace Bullying on Victims and Witnesses

Physical And Mental Health Effects on Victims of Workplace Bullying:

Workplace bullying is a serious issue that can have a significant impact on an individual's physical and mental health. Victims of workplace bullying often experience a range of negative health effects, including stress, anxiety, depression, and post-traumatic stress disorder (PTSD).

Stress is one of the most common physical health effects of workplace bullying. This is because individuals who are bullied at work feel constantly on edge, as they are unsure when the next incident will occur. This chronic stress can lead to many health problems, including high blood pressure, heart disease, and other chronic illnesses.

Victims of workplace bullying also often experience anxiety, which can manifest as constant worry or fear about returning to work. This anxiety can be so severe that some individuals may avoid going to work, leading to more stress and financial problems.

Depression is another mental health effect of workplace bullying. Employees who are bullied at work often feel isolated and alone and can struggle to have positive relationships with colleagues. This can lead to a sense of hopelessness and despair, which can be difficult to shake.

Finally, victims of workplace bullying are also at increased risk of developing PTSD. This is because the constant stress and anxiety associated with being bullied at work can lead to a sense of helplessness and a feeling of being trapped. Over time, this can result in the development of PTSD symptoms such as nightmares, flashbacks, and hypervigilance.

Overall, workplace bullying can have a significant impact on an individual's physical and mental health. Employers must try to prevent workplace bullying and provide support for employees affected by it. This can include counseling, employee assistance programs, and other resources designed to promote well-being in the workplace.

Financial Implications for Victims:

Victims of various crimes often suffer severe financial implications that can have a significant impact on their lives. These financial implications include lost productivity, medical bills, and potential job loss, among others.

First, victims of crimes may experience lost productivity due to the aftermath of an incident. For example, a victim of a car accident may have to take time off work to recover from injuries sustained in the accident. This time off work can result in lost wages, which can affect the victim's financial stability.

Second, the medical bills associated with treating injuries sustained from a crime can be substantial. Victims may require hospitalization, surgery, medication, and rehabilitation services, leading to significant expenses. Sometimes, the cost of medical treatment can be so high that the victim may not afford it, leading to further financial strain.

Finally, victims may experience potential job loss due to the physical or psychological impact of their trauma. For example, a victim of sexual assault may experience difficulty continuing to work due to the resulting trauma. Additionally, they may be unable to maintain a steady job due to flashbacks, anxiety, or depression related to the crime.

The financial implications of being a victim of a crime can be significant and far-reaching, leading to lost productivity, medical bills, and potential job loss, among others. The effects of these financial implications can further exacerbate the already traumatic experience of being a victim of a crime.

Impact Of Workplace Bullying on Witnesses:

Workplace bullying can have a far-reaching impact not only on the target, but also on witnesses forced to bear witness to this behavior. The effect of bullying on witnesses is often overlooked, but research suggests that they may suffer from feelings of guilt, shame, and anxiety about potentially becoming a victim themselves.

Witnesses of bullying may feel guilty for not intervening or speaking out against the behavior. They may feel like they didn't do enough to protect the target, and that they were complicit in allowing the bullying to occur. Seeing someone being mistreated can also trigger feelings of shame, as witnesses may feel like they are responsible for the behavior of their colleagues.

In addition, witnesses of bullying may experience heightened anxiety about becoming a target themselves. They may worry that the behavior will escalate, and that they could become the next victim. This fear can affect their work performance, leading to decreased productivity and increased absenteeism.

The psychological impact of workplace bullying on witnesses underscores the importance of addressing this behavior in the workplace. Employers should take steps to prevent bullying, offer support to those who have seen or experienced it, and create a culture of respect and kindness in the workplace.

Workplace bullying not only affects the target but has a wide-ranging impact on witnesses. These effects can manifest as feelings of guilt, shame, and anxiety about their own potential victimization. Employers must take the necessary steps to stop bullying and create a safe and respectful workplace culture for all employees.

The Importance of Support Networks for Victims & Witnesses:

Support networks for victims and witnesses are crucial for their well-being and recovery after a traumatic event. These networks can provide emotional, practical, and legal support essential for victims and witnesses to cope with the aftermath of a crime.

Counseling is an integral part of victim support networks. Victims of crimes may experience a range of emotions such as anger, anxiety, depression, and fear. Counseling provides an outlet for these emotions and helps victims to process their trauma in a healthy way. Counseling may also help victims to develop coping mechanisms, improve their self-esteem, and rebuild their confidence after an incident.

Legal resources are also vital for victims and witnesses. Legal resources offer information on the legal processes involved in prosecuting a crime and provide advocacy and assistance in navigating the legal system. Victims and witnesses may also require legal advice on issues such as obtaining protective orders, financial help, and compensation for physical, emotional, and financial damages resulting from the crime.

Support networks for victims and witnesses are fundamental to their recovery and ability to move forward after a traumatic event.

Counseling and legal resources provide vital support that can help victims and witnesses to heal, achieve justice, and regain control of their lives. It is important that these resources are accessible and available to all victims and witnesses.

Potential For Workplace Bullying to Lead to A Toxic Culture and Decreased Employee Morale & Engagement:

Workplace bullying can have devastating effects on both individuals and the entire culture of an organization. When employees are subjected to bullying behavior by their colleagues or superiors, it can create a toxic work environment that breeds fear, anxiety, and stress. This atmosphere can have a serious impact on employee morale and engagement, leading to feelings of disengagement, low motivation, and reduced productivity.

Bullied employees often feel isolated, powerless, and unsupported, leading to a range of negative outcomes for both employees and the organization. They may find it difficult to concentrate, make decisions, or solve problems. They may withdraw from social interactions, leading to further isolation and feelings of loneliness. Over time, this behavior can cause mental health issues, such as depression, anxiety, and even PTSD.

If not addressed, workplace bullying can lead to a breakdown in communication between employees, their managers, and the leadership of the organization. It can create a culture of distrust and resentment that jeopardizes teamwork and collaboration. This toxic environment can also lead to higher levels of absenteeism, employee turnover, and lower productivity, which can affect the bottom line of the organization in the long run.

To prevent the potentially disastrous effects of bullying, organizations need to foster a culture of respect, empathy, and inclusion. This means taking seriously all reports of bullying behavior and creating clear policies and procedures for addressing any incidents that occur.

Leaders must be trained to recognize and respond to bullying and other forms of abusive behavior, and managers must be held accountable for the well-being of their employees.

Workplace bullying can be damaging to individuals, teams, and organizations. By understanding the potential for damage to morale, engagement, and productivity, companies can take proactive steps to prevent this behavior and support healthier, more positive work environments.

The Legal Implications of Workplace Bullying

Workplace bullying is a significant issue that can have severe legal implications for both the individual and the company. Employees have the right to work in an environment free from bullying and harassment, and employers must ensure that their employees are not subjected to such behavior.

Employers who fail to take appropriate action against workplace bullying may face legal action, including discrimination claims or lawsuits. If a company is found to have condoned or even encouraged this behavior, courts may award substantial damages to the employee who was victimized.

Disciplinary actions for perpetrators of workplace bullying can include warnings, suspension, termination, or legal action depending on the severity of the situation. HR may also have to conduct an investigation into allegations of bullying, which can be time-consuming and costly.

Ultimately, the legal implications of workplace bullying can be serious and far-reaching. Addressing and preventing bullying in the workplace is not only the morally correct thing to do, but companies must also avoid legal and financial repercussions.

Strategies For Preventing & Addressing Workplace Bullying:

Workplace bullying is a serious issue that can negatively affect employees, reducing their productivity and job satisfaction. To prevent and address workplace bullying effectively, companies must put clear policies into practice, training programs, and communication channels for reporting incidents. Here are strategies that companies can use to prevent and address workplace bullying:

1. Develop a Clear Policy

Businesses should develop a clear policy that defines what constitutes bullying.

The policy should also outline the consequences of engaging in bullying behavior and the procedures for addressing complaints.

2. Train Employees and Managers

The business should offer training programs for employees and managers on how to recognize and prevent bullying behavior.

These training programs should also equip managers with tools and techniques for dealing with complaints and reporting procedures.

3. Establish a Safe Reporting System

Employees should feel encouraged to report workplace bullying they have experienced or witnessed. A system should be set up that lets employees report incidences of bullying without fear of retaliation.

The reporting system should be clear, easy to use, confidential, and easily accessible to all employees.

. . .

4. Address Complaints Promptly and Seriously

When a complaint is made, the business should take it seriously and act promptly. A thorough investigation should be carried out to determine the facts, and appropriate actions should be taken under the policy.

5. Foster a Positive Workplace Culture

Creating a positive workplace culture that promotes respect, inclusion, and open communication can go a long way in preventing workplace bullying.

Leaders must set an example of treating everyone with respect and fairness.

Preventing and addressing workplace bullying requires a concerted effort from everyone in the organization. By putting clear policies into practice, training programs, and reporting systems, and fostering a positive workplace culture, companies can effectively manage and prevent incidences of bullying while creating a healthy work environment.

Workplace bullying is a widespread problem that has significant negative impacts on both victims and witnesses of this behavior. Workplace bullying refers to the repetitive, needless use of power to abuse, threaten or harm another individual in a workplace setting. Victims of workplace bullying may experience a range of emotional, physical, and performance-related impacts that can affect their overall well-being and job satisfaction. Meanwhile, witnesses of this behavior are indirectly affected by the consequences of workplace bullying and can also endure negative consequences as well.

The impacts of workplace bullying on victims can be severe and long-lasting. Victims may feel constantly anxious, frustrated, and insecure. They may experience physical effects, such as headaches, digestive problems, nausea or fatigue. These effects can result in an increased interest in sick days and decreased levels of job satisfaction. In addition, victims may experience a decrease in productivity or performance in the workplace. They may feel unable to carry out their jobs or accomplish tasks to the best of their abilities, leading to a decrease in overall productivity and a reduction in the quality of work produced.

Workplace bullying can lead to long-term mental health issues that could be dangerous. Victims may develop depression, anxiety, PTSD and other serious psychological problems. A victim's self-worth and confidence may decrease significantly, leading to long-term mental health issues that could potentially become dangerous, even leading to suicidal outcomes in some cases.

Witnesses to workplace bullying may also be negatively impacted. They often experience feelings of guilt or helplessness witnessing the bullying. They may face ethical dilemmas and some-times feel obliged to help the victim, but they also face risk, such as being bullied themselves or losing their job over interfering in the matter. Ultimately, witnesses may suffer from work stress, anxiety or depression and can harm their productivity level, job performance, and mental well-being.

To conclude, workplace bullying has serious negative conse-quences for both victims and witnesses. It can lead to emotional distress, physical problems, and reduced productivity or work perfor-mance. It can also have long-term negative effects on mental health, which might increase the risk of suicidal behaviors in extreme cases. Organizations must develop and implement workplace policies to eliminate such negative behaviors to create a healthy, productive work environment that is welcoming, respectful and encouraging of all employees.

The Psychological Effects of Workplace Bullying on Victims & Witnesses:

Workplace bullying is a form of mistreatment that can have serious psychological effects on its victims and witnesses. It involves the repeated and intentional targeting of an individual with negative behaviors such as humiliation, intimidation, and belittlement, among others.

Victims of workplace bullying often develop symptoms of depression, anxiety, and post-traumatic stress disorder (PTSD). Depression is a mood disorder characterized by feelings of sadness, loneliness, and loss of interest in activities that were once enjoyable. Individuals bullied at work may feel low self-esteem, hopeless, and struggle to cope with their emotions.

Anxiety, on the other hand, is a feeling of unease, such as worry or fear, that can be mild or severe. The prolonged stress that comes with workplace bullying can lead to anxiety disorders, which can debilitate and impact various parts of one's life, both personally and professionally.

PTSD is a condition that can occur because of experiencing or witnessing a traumatic event. It is most often associated with military combat, but it can also happen following workplace bullying. It can cause nightmares, flashbacks, and avoidance behavior, among other symptoms, which can seriously affect one's emotional and psychological well-being.

Witnesses of workplace bullying can also experience psychological trauma. They may feel guilt for not stopping the bullying and fear they may also become targets in the future.

Workplace bullying can have significant negative consequences on both victims and witnesses, leading to depression, anxiety, and PTSD, among other psychological effects. Organizations must have policies in place to combat workplace bullying and create a supportive work environment for all employees.

Rae A. Stonehouse

* * *

The Impact Of Workplace Bullying On Productivity And Overall Organizational Success

The Impact of Workplace Bullying on Productivity & Organizational Success:

Definition & Types of Workplace Bullying:

Workplace bullying refers to the continual and intentional mistreatment of one or more employees by an individual or a group at the workplace. It can take various forms, including verbal abuse, physical aggression, and emotional manipulation.

Verbal bullying involves the use of language to humiliate, intimidate, or belittle a colleague. It may include ridiculing, shouting, threats, or spreading false rumors about an individual in the workplace.

Physical bullying involves using physical force or the threat of bodily harm to intimidate or harm a coworker. It may include physical attacks, destruction of property, or unwanted touching.

Emotional bullying involves manipulative behaviors that create a hostile and unhealthy work environment. It includes behaviors such as scapegoating, undermining, and withholding information or resources.

Workplace bullying not only negatively affects the individuals who experience it but also affects the entire organization's morale, productivity, and success. It can lead to decreased job satisfaction, higher turnover rates, reduced performance, and increased absenteeism. So it is essential to recognize and address workplace bullying to create a safe and healthy work environment for all employees.

Effects Of Workplace Bullying on Employee Productivity:

Workplace bullying can have serious negative effects on an employee's productivity, job satisfaction, and mental well-being. When an employee is subjected to bullying, they may feel demoralized and powerless, which can lead to decreased motivation and productivity. This is because they may feel that their work is not valued or appreciated, and their efforts may go unrecognized. They may become disengaged from their work and start to withdraw from their coworkers and the organization.

Workplace bullying can also affect an employee's job satisfaction. Being bullied can cause a sense of frustration, anxiety, and a feeling of being undervalued. Employees who feel they are being treated unfairly or subjected to abusive behavior may become dissatisfied with their work, which can lead to absenteeism, turnover, and reduced productivity.

Workplace bullying can also lead to significant mental health problems such as depression, anxiety, and post-traumatic stress disorder (PTSD). Employees who endure workplace bullying may experience high levels of stress, have trouble sleeping, and may even experience physical symptoms such as headaches and stomachaches. As a result, their mental well-being is impaired, which can further influence their overall performance at work.

Workplace bullying is a significant issue that can have far-reaching negative effects on an employee's productivity, job satisfaction, and mental well-being. It is important for organizations to take steps to prevent and address bullying in the workplace to create a healthy and productive work environment. By creating policies and procedures that address workplace bullying, organizations can help prevent and deter this behavior and create a more respectful, positive, and productive workplace culture.

Costs Of Employee Morale & Turnover:

Workplace bullying is not only harmful to the individual being bullied but also to the organization. Bullying can have significant costs to employee morale, turnover rates and ultimately affect the financial health of an organization.

Employee Morale: Workplace bullying can cause low morale among employees. It creates a hostile work environment, causing employees to feel demotivated and disengaged. Employees are less likely to feel good about their job when they don't feel safe or supported, leading to decreased productivity and often causing them to take more sick leave and ultimately reduce their commitment to the organization.

Turnover Rates: Bullying can result in an increase in turnover rates, as employees are likely to leave the organization due to the negative experience. The high cost of recruitment, training, and loss of talent can have a significant impact on the organization's financial health.

. . .

Costs to the Organization: The costs associated with workplace bullying can be substantial. There are legal costs in the form of claims or lawsuits, but equally important is the real loss of productivity, reduced work quality and reduced employee engagement. Workplace bullying can also lead to reputational damage and have a long-lasting impact on organizational culture.

Workplace bullying can lead to high costs for the organization in terms of employee turnover and low morale, ultimately affecting the financial health of the company. Organizations must take proactive steps to address and prevent the insidious effects of bullying on employees to establish a working environment based on fairness and respect for all. Employees who feel valued, supported, and safe are much more likely to perform at their best, ultimately having a positive impact on the organization's success.

Bullied Employees' Behavioral & Coping Mechanisms:

Bullying in the workplace is an unfortunate reality, and it can take a serious toll on the mental and emotional health of its victims. While the effects of bullying can vary significantly from one person to the next, there are common behavioral and coping mechanisms that bullied employees may use to deal with the situation.

First, many victims of bullying may try to avoid the bully or the situation altogether. They may start to avoid work or social events or even quit their job altogether to escape harassment. While avoidance can provide some temporary relief, it is not an effective long-term solution, and it can even make the situation worse by causing the victim to feel isolated and disconnected from their colleagues and the workplace.

Another coping mechanism that bullied employees may use is to try to confront the bully directly. They may try to stand up for themselves, call out the bully's behavior or seek help from colleagues or human resources. While this can be an effective way to take control of the situation, it can also be risky, as it may lead to further retaliation or a worsening of bullying behavior.

A third coping mechanism often used by victims of bullying is to seek support from friends, family, or a professional counselor. This can be an effective way to process the emotions and feelings associated with being bullied and to develop a plan for moving forward based on self-care and resilience-building.

Overall, the most effective coping mechanism for bullied employees is likely to be a combination of several strategies. This may include seeking social support, developing assertiveness and communication skills, and working with a mental health professional to address the emotional and psychological effects of bullying. With the right coping mechanisms in place, bullied employees can regain their control and confidence, and take positive steps toward creating a healthier and happier workplace environment.

Organizational Policies & Procedures to Counter Bullying:

Bullying in the workplace is a serious issue that can hurt employee morale and productivity and lead to increased absenteeism and high turnover rates. To counter bullying, organizations can implement the following policies and procedures:

1. Clear communication and awareness: Organizations should clearly communicate the consequences of bullying to all employees and make them aware of behaviors that are unacceptable. This can be achieved through training and communication programs.

2. Zero tolerance policy: Organizations should implement a zero-tolerance policy for bullying in the workplace. The policy should outline clear consequences for bullying, and make sure all employees are aware of the policy.

3. Complaint mechanisms: The organization should have an effective complaint mechanism in place that employees can use to report incidents of bullying without fear of retaliation. The mechanism should be confidential, and the organization should take appropriate action to investigate and resolve complaints.

4. Support systems: Organizations should provide support systems for employees who have been bullied, such as counseling and mental health services. These support systems can be helped with through Employee Assistance Programs (EAPs).

5. Regular tracking and review: The organization should regularly track and review its policies and procedures on bullying to ensure they are effective and being implemented. This can be achieved through feedback from employees, surveys, and audits.

Organizations play a key role in creating a healthy work environment free of bullying. By putting policies and procedures into practice that promote awareness, clear communication, and employee support, organizations can effectively counter bullying in the workplace.

The Role of Leadership in Preventing Workplace Bullying:

Leadership plays a crucial role in preventing workplace bullying. Organizational leaders are responsible for creating a safe and inclusive work environment that nurtures and supports employees, and preventing bullying is a critical part of this responsibility. By setting the tone for the workplace culture, leaders can create an environment that promotes respect, kindness, and collaboration among employees, while discouraging any abusive behavior.

Effective leaders understand the importance of maintaining an open dialogue with employees, which helps them to identify and address any concerns related to bullying in the workplace. Leaders must also work to establish a code of conduct that clearly outlines the expectations for behavior in the workplace, and this should include specific policies related to harassment, discrimination, and bullying. These policies should be regularly communicated to employees to make sure everyone is aware of the organization's stance.

In addition to setting policies and communicating expectations, leaders must also commit to fostering a culture of respect and inclusivity. This means promoting diversity and welcoming differences among employees, while also creating a sense of empowerment and belonging for all individuals. Leaders who focus on the well-being and happiness of their employees can effectively prevent and address any incidents of bullying and will create an environment that is both productive and fulfilling for everyone involved.

The role of leadership in preventing workplace bullying is critical. By creating an inclusive and supportive work environment, setting clear expectations and policies, and focusing on the well-being of employees, leaders can effectively prevent bullying and promote a culture of respect and collaboration. By working together to create a safe and happy workplace, leaders can make sure their organizations thrive and their employees succeed.

Case Studies of Organizations That Have Tackled Workplace Bullying:

Case Study One: Google

In 2018, Google underwent an investigation into allegations of workplace bullying, specifically sexual harassment and discrimination. Over 20,000 employees walked out in protest, demanding changes in the company's approach to dealing with these issues. As a result, Google put several measures into practice to improve its policies, including an end to forced arbitration for all employee claims of sexual harassment, more transparency in reporting, and better support for employees who report such incidents.

Outcome: Google's actions were praised for being swift and effective in addressing workplace bullying. The company's efforts were dubbed a "watershed moment" in the tech industry's battle against harassment and discrimination.

Lesson learned: Swift and sweeping changes, paired with a visible stand against bullying and harassment, can change the company's culture and be a catalyst for positive change in the industry.

Case Study Two: Royal Mail

The Royal Mail faced accusations of toxic working cultures and extreme behavior such as name-calling, public shaming, and aggressive language, which led to 8,000 complaints of workplace bullying. The company launched a campaign to address the issue, including setting up an investigation team, creating a confidential hotline for reporting complaints, and offering guidance and support to managers to help build positive workplace cultures.

Outcome: The company's approach yielded positive results, with a 22% drop in complaints regarding bullying and harassment, according to its annual report.

. . .

Lesson learned: Providing a confidential reporting mechanism and tracking has an important role in preventing workplace bullying. Training of managers and other senior employees can also be critical in preventing incidents of workplace bullying and setting the tone for a positive work culture.

Case Study Three: DreamWorks Animation

DreamWorks Animation was accused by a female executive of workplace bullying, retaliation after she reported misconduct, and gender discrimination. The company's CEO called for an investigation and later stepped down from his position. DreamWorks started changes that included increased training of employees across all levels on workplace bullying and harassment, expanding its HR team to help with reporting and complaints management, and redesigning the company's policies and reporting channels to promote greater transparency in reporting and communication.

Outcome: The outcome is still ongoing, but the company's approach to the accusations was being watched closely by the entertainment industry, which has been grappling with allegations of workplace harassment and bullying.

Lesson learned: When dealing with allegations of workplace bullying and harassment, companies must take their response seriously, investigate, and communicate transparently with their employees. Promoting behavior that values respect and accountability for all employees regardless of gender, race, or any other characteristic is vital.

Workplace bullying can have a significant impact on productivity and organizational success, leading to a decrease in employee morale and an increase in turnover. When employees are bullied at work, they tend to feel demoralized, isolated, and overwhelmed, which can result in decreased motivation, job satisfaction, and work performance. Ultimately, this can lead to lost productivity, lower quality work, and missed deadlines.

One significant cost of workplace bullying is the damage it can cause to employee morale. When employees feel unsupported, unappreciated or unvalued, they are more likely to become disengaged from their work, leading to decreased productivity, increased absenteeism, and higher employee turnover. This can also result in a negative impact on the overall culture of an organization, leading to a more toxic work environment and damaging a company's reputation.

Another cost of workplace bullying is the impact it can have on employee retention. When employees are subjected to persistent and unaddressed bullying behavior, they may leave the organization. This can cause a loss of skilled employees, which can affect the overall success of the organization.

Organizations that do not address workplace bullying may also suffer from increased costs associated with legal action, decreased productivity, increased health and safety incidents, and increased absenteeism.

Workplace bullying can have harmful effects on both employees and organizations. Addressing and preventing workplace bullying should be a priority for any organization that wishes to maintain productivity, employee morale, and organizational success.

* * *

The Legal And Ethical Implications Of Workplace Bullying

The Legal Framework and Regulatory Requirements for Preventing & Addressing Workplace Bullying

Overview Of Workplace Bullying and Its Impact on Individuals & Organizations:

W orkplace bullying is defined as repeated and deliberate mistreatment of an individual by a colleague or superior in the workplace. It can take many forms, including verbal, physical, or psychological abuse, and can have serious consequences for both individuals and organizations.

Research has shown that workplace bullying can have a significant negative impact on the mental health and well-being of individuals. Victims of workplace bullying may experience increased levels of stress, anxiety, and depression, which can lead to poor job performance and absenteeism. In severe cases, workplace bullying may even lead to post-traumatic stress disorder (PTSD).

The impact of workplace bullying is not limited to individual employees. It can also have a ripple effect on the organization. Workplace bullying can create a toxic working environment, decrease job satisfaction, and lead to high turnover rates. It can also harm the organization's reputation, leading to a loss of trust and credibility among employees, customers, and stakeholders.

In addition, workplace bullying can have financial implications for organizations. Employees who are victims of workplace bullying may require medical treatment or counseling, leading to increased healthcare costs. There may also be legal costs associated with defending against claims of workplace bullying.

To prevent workplace bullying, organizations can put policies and procedures into practice that make it clear that bullying behavior will not be tolerated. This can include training for managers and employees on how to recognize and prevent workplace bullying and channels for employees to report incidents of bullying. By focusing on a safe and respectful workplace culture, organizations can promote employee well-being, job satisfaction, and productivity while preventing the negative impacts of workplace bullying.

Legal Framework for Preventing & Addressing Workplace Bullying:

The prevention and addressing of workplace bullying in the United States is governed by a set of laws, regulations, and guidelines. The legal framework includes several federal and state laws that provide protections to employees against bullying at the workplace.

The main federal law governing workplace bullying is the Occupational Safety and Health Act of 1970 (OSHA). According to OSHA, employers have a legal responsibility to ensure a safe and healthy work environment free from any form of bullying or harassment. In addition, the Civil Rights Act of 1964 prohibits workplace harassment or discrimination based on race, sex, religion, color, or national origin.

The Americans with Disabilities Act of 1990 (ADA) prohibits discrimination against individuals with disabilities in the workplace, including bullying. Similarly, the Age Discrimination in Employment Act of 1967 (ADEA) protects employees aged 40 and higher from bullying and harassment due to their age.

Several states have also passed their own anti-bullying laws, which provide more protections to employees. For example, California has the Workplace Violence Prevention in Health Care standard, which requires healthcare employers to implement and maintain an effective workplace violence prevention plan. Several states, including California, Massachusetts, and Washington, have also passed anti-bullying legislation that requires employers to develop policies and procedures for addressing workplace bullying.

In addition to these laws and regulations, several organizations have developed guidelines for preventing and addressing workplace bullying. For example, the Occupational Safety and Health Administration (OSHA) has issued guidelines on preventing workplace violence, while the Society for Human Resource Management (SHRM) has developed a toolkit for employers to prevent and address bullying at the workplace.

The legal framework for preventing and addressing workplace bullying includes federal and state laws, guidelines, and regulations that provide protections to employees. Employers must know these laws and make sure their policies and procedures for preventing and addressing workplace bullying comply with them.

Obligations And Responsibilities of Employers and Employees In Preventing & Addressing Workplace Bullying:

Workplace bullying is a serious matter that needs to be prevented and addressed by both employers and employees. Here are obligations and responsibilities that employers and employees should uphold to prevent and address workplace bullying:

. . .

Employers' Obligations and Responsibilities:

1. Establish a clear anti-bullying policy - Employers must have an anti-bullying policy in place that defines what workplace bullying is, and what steps employees can take if they experience or witness bullying.

2. Provide training to employees - Employers must provide training to all employees on how to recognize and report workplace bullying and how to handle conflicts in the workplace.

3. Take complaints seriously - Employers must take all complaints of workplace bullying seriously, thoroughly investigate and take appropriate actions.

4. Create a safe work environment - Employers must make sure the workplace is a safe environment for all employees, free from harassment or bullying.

5. Follow up - Employers must follow up on any complaints or incidents of workplace bullying, to make sure the problem has been resolved and that employees feel safe.

Employees' Obligations and Responsibilities:

. . .

1. Treat colleagues with respect - Employees must treat their colleagues with respect and should not engage in any behavior that could be perceived as bullying.

2. Report bullying - Employees should report any incidents of bullying they experience or witness to their supervisor or HR department.

3. Be a supportive bystander - Employees should support colleagues being bullied, by offering to help them or by reporting the bullying on their behalf.

4. Cooperate with investigations - Employees should cooperate with any investigations into workplace bullying, providing honest and accurate information.

5. Respect confidentiality - Employees should respect the confidentiality of any complaint or investigation related to workplace bullying and should not discuss it with others without permission.

By upholding these obligations and responsibilities, employers and employees can work together to prevent and address workplace bullying, creating a safe and respectful work environment for all.

Best Practices for Creating and Implementing Anti-Bullying Policies & Procedures in The Workplace:

1. Involve Employees: Involve employees in the development of policies and procedures. Gather input from everyone and use it to create a comprehensive anti-bullying policy that reflects your workforce values.

. . .

2. Training and Education: Provide training and education for all employees on the types of behavior that can be considered bullying, how to report it, and the consequences.

3. Reporting processes: Create an accessible reporting process that employees can use. They should feel safe and able to report bullying without fear of retaliation.

4. Investigation and Resolution: Designate an impartial person or team to investigate reports of bullying using a standard protocol. Provide clear guidance on the steps that will be taken to resolve the situation and follow up with the employee.

5. Accountability and Consequences: Clearly communicate that bullying behavior will not be tolerated, and make sure real consequences are enforced when incidents occur.

6. Ongoing review and refinement: Monitor your policies and procedures continually, make necessary updates and continuously assess the impact of the policy on your workplace.

Overall, creating and implementing anti-bullying policies and procedures requires collaboration, education, communication, and reinforcement to succeed. An effective system should promote the safety and well-being of all employees while reducing incidents during the work process.

Role Of Organizational Culture and Leadership in Preventing & Addressing Workplace Bullying:

Organizational culture and leadership play a crucial role in preventing and addressing workplace bullying. Here are five ways how:

1. Value of Respect and Inclusivity: An organizational culture that promotes respect, inclusivity and collaboration can prevent and reduce the incidence of workplace bullying. Leadership can establish codes of conduct that promote positive behavior, emphasizing the importance of respect for all employees.

2. Clear Policies: Strong anti-bullying policies with clear procedures for reporting and investigating any incidents of bullying can help deter bullying. The leadership should communicate these policies often and create a safe environment where employees can come forward and report the issues.

3. Training and Awareness: Providing regular training on recognizing and addressing bullying behavior helps employees identify the meaning of bullying and its impact. Leadership should be committed to raising awareness and providing the necessary training, so employees know how to avoid, address and report any incident of bullying.

4. Accountability: Creating a culture of accountability where bullying is not tolerated, and individuals who perpetrate bullying or fail to speak out against it are held accountable is critical. Leaders should take every report of bullying seriously, investigate it properly, and take appropriate action against the perpetrator.

5. Empowerment: Leadership can empower employees and involve them in creating a positive and supportive workplace. This will enable employees to feel safe to talk about their experiences and suggest preventing or mitigate the effects of bullying. When employees feel supported, appreciated, and have a sense of belonging, the likelihood of bullying incidents significantly reduces.

Preventing and addressing workplace bullying requires a joint effort of leadership and the organization's culture. By creating an inclusive and respectful environment, clear policies, training, accountability and empowerment, leadership can help to foster a workplace free from bullying and its negative impact.

Effective Strategies for Investigating & Responding to Workplace Bullying Allegations:

Workplace bullying can have a major impact on an organization's culture and its employees' mental health, job satisfaction, and productivity. So, organizations need to have effective strategies in place for investigating and responding to workplace bullying allegations. Here are six strategies that can be helpful:

1. Develop clear policies: An effective way to prevent bullying is to have clear policies in place that define bullying and lay out the consequences for perpetrators. Providing employees with a clear understanding of what is considered bullying makes it easier for them to report incidents when they occur.

. . .

2. Encourage reporting: Create a reporting process that is easy to use, confidential, non-retaliatory, and supportive. Train employees on how to report bullying incidents, and make sure they understand that all reports will be taken seriously.

3. Conduct timely and thorough investigations: Once an incident has been reported, it is important to conduct a timely and thorough investigation. The investigation should be objective, fair, and conducted by a knowledgeable and impartial investigator.

4. Take corrective action: If an investigation determines that bullying occurred, organizations should take corrective action to address it. This could include taking disciplinary action against the perpetrator, providing support to the victim, or developing a plan to prevent future incidents.

5. Provide support: Provide support to victims of bullying, including access to counseling, legal assistance, and employee assistance programs. Also, provide training to managers and employees on how to recognize and prevent bullying.

6. Monitor and evaluate: Regularly track and evaluate the effectiveness of the organization's anti-bullying policies and procedures. Survey employees to determine if they feel safe and respected in the workplace, and measure changes in the organization's culture.

Importance Of Ongoing Monitoring & Evaluation of Anti-Bullying Efforts in The Workplace:

Bullying is a serious issue in the workplace that affects the morale and productivity of employees. Anti-bullying efforts aim to prevent and stop bullying behavior. Ongoing tracking and evaluation of these efforts are essential to ensuring their effectiveness. Here are reasons why ongoing tracking and evaluation of anti-bullying efforts in the workplace are important:

1. Detection of new forms of bullying: Bullies can be creative in their tactics, and their behavior can evolve. Ongoing tracking and evaluation can help identify new forms of bullying behaviors that may not have been seen before. By detecting these behaviors early, organizations can try to address them before they escalate.

2. Identification of gaps in policies and procedures: Regular monitoring lets the organization identify weaknesses in their anti-bullying policies and procedures. By evaluating where these gaps exist, organizations can work to strengthen their policies and procedures to better address new or existing bullying situations.

3. Measuring effectiveness: Monitoring, and evaluation provide feedback on the effectiveness of the efforts to prevent bullying in the workplace. If an organization is not seeing a significant improvement in workplace culture and employee morale, or if there's an increase in the number of bullying incidents, it may show that the current anti-bullying efforts are not effective. Regular tracking can help compare the situation before and after implementing the anti-bullying efforts.

4. Providing evidence for continued support: Monitoring and evaluation provide the evidence needed to show the effectiveness of anti-bullying efforts to management, employees, and stakeholders. Having this evidence lets organizations advocate for continued support and investment in anti-bullying programs.

5. Enhancing accountability: Monitoring and evaluating anti-bullying efforts can increase accountability across the organization. Regular evaluation and feedback mechanisms reinforce the idea that the organization is committed to preventing bullying while holding responsible parties accountable for their actions. It also allows employees to report any incidents openly and safely they face or witness.

Ongoing monitoring and evaluation of anti-bullying efforts in the workplace are crucial in making sure employees feel safe, secure, and comfortable, thus enhancing productivity and overall organizational performance. Through continuous evaluation, management can address gaps in policies and procedures, respond more effectively to bullying incidents, and cultivate a supportive work environment.

Workplace bullying is a serious issue that negatively affects the physical and emotional well-being of individuals and organizations. Legal frameworks and regulatory requirements have been put in place to protect employees from bullying and harassment in the workplace. This essay discusses the background, legal framework, and regulatory requirements for preventing and addressing work-place bullying.

Background

Workplace bullying is a form of psychological violence that includes behaviors such as intimidation, humiliation, and exclusion.

It can occur through physical, verbal, or nonverbal actions, and can have severe consequences for the individual's mental, emotional, and physical health. In recent years, governments, organizations, and individuals have become increasingly aware of the impact of workplace bullying, resulting in policies and guidelines aimed at preventing and addressing this issue.

Legal Framework

In the United States, there is currently no federal law that specifically targets workplace bullying, but that does not mean there are no laws or regulations put into place to address it. Several laws aimed at protecting employees from harassment, discrimination, and other forms of mistreatment in the workplace also cover bullying. These include Title VII of the Civil Rights Act of 1964, the Americans with Disabilities Act, the Age Discrimination in Employment Act, and the National Labor Relations Act.

Title VII of the Civil Rights Act of 1964 is a federal law that prohibits employment discrimination based on race, color, religion, sex, or national origin. It covers discrimination in hiring, firing, promotions, and other employment-related issues. Workplace bullying can be considered a form of discrimination or harassment, which can lead to lawsuits and penalties for employers who fail to address it.

The Americans with Disabilities Act is a federal law that prohibits discrimination against individuals with disabilities in the workplace. It requires employers to provide reasonable accommodations for employees with disabilities and to refrain from harassment or discrimination against them.

The Age Discrimination in Employment Act is a federal law that protects employees 40 years or older from discrimination in the workplace. This law prohibits age-based harassment, discrimination in hiring, firing, and other employment-related actions based on age.

The National Labor Relations Act is a federal law that protects employees' right to organize, unionize, and engage in collective bargaining. This law also prohibits employers from interfering with employees' rights and from retaliating against employees who engage in protected concerted activities.

Regulatory Requirements

In addition to federal laws, regulatory requirements dictate how employers should handle workplace bullying. The Occupational Safety and Health Administration (OSHA) states that employers must provide a safe and healthy workplace free from recognized hazards. Workplace bullying can be considered a hazard that can negatively affect employees' mental and emotional well-being, therefore making it the employers' responsibility to provide a safe and healthy workplace free from workplace bullying.

The Equal Employment Opportunity Commission (EEOC) also provides guidelines for preventing and addressing workplace bullying. These guidelines state that employers should have policies and procedures in place that prohibit, and address workplace bullying, investigate complaints, and prevent and remedy bullying.

Workplace bullying is a serious issue that affects the health and well-being of employees and organizations. Legal frameworks and regulatory requirements have been put in place to protect employees from workplace bullying. While the United States does not have a specific law for workplace bullying, several laws that protect employees from harassment, discrimination, and other forms of mistreatment also cover workplace bullying. Employers should also put policies and procedures into practice aimed at preventing and addressing workplace bullying to create a healthy, safe, and inclusive workplace for all employees.

An Overview of Relevant OH&S Legislation & Regulations:

Introduction To Occupational Health and Safety (OH&S) Legislation & Regulations:

Occupational Health and Safety (OH&S) legislation and regulations are laws and regulations designed to promote a safe and healthy working environment for employees in various workplaces. These laws and regulations are put in place to maintain safe working conditions, to reduce the risk of workplace accidents, injuries, and fatalities, and to protect the well-being of workers.

The OH&S legislation and regulations focus on promoting the health and safety of workers in different industries such as construction, manufacturing, mining, and healthcare. The laws require employers to take measures to prevent workplace accidents and injuries, such as providing proper training, maintaining safe equipment and facilities, and implementing safety protocols.

In addition, the OH&S regulations require employers to provide adequate personal protective equipment (PPE) to their employees and to regularly assess and monitor workplace hazards, to make sure workers are not exposed to any harm. Failure to comply with these regulations can result in serious consequences, including hefty fines, closure of the workplace, and even imprisonment.

OH&S legislation and regulations play a crucial role in making sure employees have the right to work in a safe and healthy environment. It is essential for both employers and employees to understand, comply and enforce these regulations to promote a safer work environment.

Explanation Of the Purpose & Scope Of OH&S Laws:

Occupational Health and Safety (OH&S) laws are designed to protect the health, safety, and welfare of workers in the workplace. The purpose of these laws is to prevent accidents, injuries, and fatalities and to make sure workers are not exposed to harmful conditions or substances. OH&S laws also aim to promote the overall well-being of workers by addressing factors that could affect their physical and mental health.

The scope of OH&S laws covers a wide range of issues related to workplace safety and health, including hazard identification and assessment, risk management and control, safety procedures and training, personal protective equipment, emergency response procedures, and reporting and investigation of accidents and incidents. OH&S laws also cover issues related to occupational health, such as workplace hygiene measures, exposure to hazardous substances, ergonomic considerations, and mental health support.

OH&S laws vary from country to country, and even from state to state or region to region within a country. However, the basic principles and goals of these laws remain the same: to ensure the safety and well-being of workers and to create a safe and healthy working environment. Overall, OH&S laws are an essential part of any modern society and contribute to the overall health and well-being of the workforce and society at large.

The Role of Government and Employers in Ensuring Compliance With OH&S Legislation:

Occupational health and safety (OH&S) legislation is designed to protect workers from work-related injuries, illnesses and deaths. To ensure compliance with these laws and regulations, both the government and employers have an important role to play. Here's a closer look at the specific responsibilities of each:

. . .

The Role of Government:

1. Enforcing OH&S Legislation - The government is responsible for enforcing workplace safety laws and regulations. The regulatory bodies, such as WorkSafe or OSHA, oversee compliance within various sectors and take necessary action if negligence or malpractice is found.

2. Educating Employers and Employees - The government can provide educational materials and resources to both employers and employees about OH&S legislation. This education can raise awareness of what is required, how to prevent dangerous situations, and how to recognize and respond to health-related situations at work.

3. **Developing and Updating Codes, Standards and Best Practices** - The government is constantly updating and developing OH&S code and regulations that govern workplace safety. Employers must adhere to these regulations and standards to make sure their workplaces are safe and healthy.

The Role of Employers:

1. Providing a Safe and Healthy Work Environment - Employers are responsible for providing a safe and healthy work environment for their employees. This includes maintaining machinery, installing safety features and providing Personal Protective Equipment (PPE).

. . .

2. Conducting Regular Workplace Inspections - Employers must implement regular workplace inspections to identify and address any OH&S hazards. Regular inspection ensures that any environmental hazards, machine abnormalities, or unsafe procedures are detected early and resolved, thus protecting the workers throughout their work hours.

3. Training and Educating Employees - Employers must provide regular employee training on the proper use of work equipment, safe working practices and other OH&S-related subjects.

Briefly, the government enforces OH&S legislation and provides education and resources, while employers must provide a safe work environment and train their employees. By working together, both can make sure workplaces stay safe, healthy, and productive.

Overview Of Key OH&S Laws & Regulations:

Occupational Health and Safety (OH&S) laws and regulations are designed to ensure the safety and well-being of workers in the workplace. These laws and regulations cover a range of topics, including health and safety standards, requirements for workplace safety procedures, and protections against workplace bullying.

One of the key pieces of legislation governing OH&S in the workplace is the Occupational Health and Safety Act (OHSA). This act sets out the general duties of employers, supervisors and workers in ensuring workplace safety. Under the OHSA, employers must make every reasonable effort to provide a safe workplace, including making sure equipment and machinery is in good working order, providing safety training to employees, and developing safety procedures and policies.

In addition to the OHSA, there are several other regulations and guidelines that relate to specific areas of workplace safety. For example, the Workplace Hazardous Materials Information System

(WHMIS) requires employers to provide information on hazardous materials used in the workplace, including safety data sheets (SDS) and labels that show the potential hazards of each material.

Another important area of OH&S regulation is the prevention of workplace bullying. Many jurisdictions have enacted legislation that specifically addresses bullying in the workplace. For example, in Ontario, the Occupational Health and Safety Act has been expanded to include provisions that require employers to take steps to prevent and address workplace harassment, including bullying. This includes developing policies and procedures to prevent bullying, providing training and education to employees, and investigating allegations of harassment or bullying.

In addition to these regulatory requirements, there are several voluntary standards and certifications that employers may adhere to. For example, the ISO 45001 standard outlines the requirements for an effective occupational health and safety management system. Adhering to this standard can help companies to show their commitment to workplace safety and may also provide additional legal protections in the event of an OH&S incident in the workplace.

Overall, OH&S laws and regulations play a critical role in ensuring the safety and well-being of workers. By understanding and complying with these regulations, employers can help to create a safe and healthy workplace environment that protects the worker.

Importance Of Risk Assessment and Management in Occupational Health & Safety Under the Law Re Bullying in The Workplace:

Risk assessment and management are essential parts of occupational health and safety, particularly when addressing bullying in the workplace. This is because bullying can have serious physical and psychological impacts on employees, leading to decreased job satisfaction, absenteeism and decreased productivity. It can also lead to various forms of harassment and discrimination, which are illegal under most countries' labor laws.

Risk assessment helps organizations to identify potential sources of bullying in the workplace, such as intolerance, aggression, disrespect, and discrimination. It determines the likelihood and severity of harm to employees and helps determine appropriate mitigation measures such as staff training, support and counseling for those affected, and policies and procedures to monitor and manage the risk of bullying.

Risk management, on the other hand, helps organizations to implement the identified mitigation measures effectively. Without risk management, it may be difficult to create an environment free of bullying, which would not comply with the law in most countries. The management of risks associated with bullying in the workplace must be approached in a systematic, proactive and continuous manner to create and sustain a positive, healthy and productive work environment.

Risk assessment and management are crucial for upholding occupational health and safety laws that regulate bullying at work. They are essential in creating an organizational culture that is zero-tolerant of bullying, encourages respect, promotes diversity, and focuses on the well-being of employees. By complying with these laws, organizations can ultimately foster a thriving workforce, enhance their brand reputation, and contribute positively to society.

OH&S Laws and Regulations in Specific Industries or Workplaces:

Bullying in the workplace is a serious issue that can affect employees' health, productivity, and overall well-being. In response to this problem, various occupational health and safety (OH&S) laws and regulations have been developed to protect workers from bullying in different industries and workplaces. Here are examples of OH&S laws and regulations related to bullying:

. . .

Construction Industry:

In the construction industry, employers have a duty of care to provide a safe and healthy workplace for all employees. This includes protecting workers from bullying and harassment. Under the Occupational Safety and Health Act 2004 (Vic), employers must provide a workplace free from risks to health and safety, including psychological risks. They must also provide information, training, and supervision to make sure their employees can work safely and without fear of bullying or harassment.

Healthcare Industry:

In the healthcare industry, bullying can have serious consequences for both employees and patients. Healthcare workers are often in high-pressure environments, and bullying can lead to increased stress and a decreased quality of patient care. To address this issue, many countries have developed specific regulations to prevent and address bullying in healthcare workplaces. For example, the Australian Nursing and Midwifery Federation has developed guidelines to prevent workplace violence and bullying in the healthcare sector, which emphasize the need for reporting and intervention when bullying occurs.

Manufacturing Industry:

In the manufacturing industry, bullying can take many forms, including physical, verbal, and emotional abuse. To prevent and address workplace bullying in this industry, employers must comply with OH&S laws and regulations. For example, in Ontario, Canada, the Occupational Health and Safety Act requires employers to protect their workers from workplace violence and harassment, including bullying. Employers must have policies and procedures in place to prevent bullying and respond to incidents when they occur.

OH&S laws and regulations are crucial in protecting workers from bullying in different industries and workplaces. Employers must understand their legal obligations and take proactive steps to prevent and address workplace bullying to create a safe and healthy work environment for all employees.

Consequences Of Non-Compliance With OH&S Regulations and Ways to Report a Breach Re Workplace Bullying:

Consequences of Non-compliance With OH&S Regulations:

- **Fines and penalties:** Organizations that do not comply with OH&S regulations can be fined and penalized by authorities. Depending on the violation, the penalties can be substantial and can harm the finances of the organization.
- **Legal liabilities:** Non-compliance with OH&S regulations can also lead to legal liabilities for the organization. Employees who suffer injuries or illnesses at work can sue the company for compensation. The organization may also have to pay for medical expenses and rehabilitation costs.
- **Loss of reputation:** Non-compliance with OH&S regulations can damage the reputation of the organization. Negative publicity can lead to the loss of customers, investors, and employees.

Ways to Report a Breach Re Workplace Bullying:

- **Reporting to supervisors:** One of the most effective ways to report a breach of workplace bullying is to report it to your immediate supervisor. He or she can take appropriate measures to address the issue.
- **HR department:** If the supervisor cannot resolve the issue, the HR department should be notified. The HR department can investigate the matter and take appropriate action.
- **Whistleblowing hotlines:** Many organizations have whistleblowing hotlines that employees can use to report breaches of workplace bullying. These hotlines are anonymous and can be used to report any unethical or illegal behavior.
- **Government agencies:** If the organization does not take appropriate action, the breach can be reported to government agencies that regulate workplace safety and employment laws. These agencies can investigate the matter and impose fines and penalties on the organization if necessary.

Occupational Health and Safety (OH&S) legislation and regulations are designed to protect workers from harm in the workplace. These laws establish requirements for employers to provide safe working conditions, and they also establish penalties for violation of safety regulations. Here are the key pieces of OH&S legislation and regulation that apply to most industries:

- **Occupational Health and Safety Act (OHSA):** OHSA is the primary legislation regulating health and safety in the workplace in most Canadian jurisdictions.

The law establishes the rights and duties of employers and workers in providing safe and healthy workplaces.

- **Workplace Hazardous Materials Information System (WHMIS):** WHMIS is a regulatory system that aims to provide workers with information about the safe use, handling, storage, and transportation of hazardous materials in the workplace. WHMIS requires employers to provide appropriate labeling, safety data sheets, and training on handling hazardous materials.
- **Canada Labour Code:** The Canada Labour Code is the main piece of legislation covering workplaces under federal jurisdiction. It sets minimum employment standards and conditions of work, as well as outlining the rights and responsibilities of workers and employers.
- **Canadian Occupational Health and Safety Regulations:** These regulations outline the specific requirements for workplace safety, including issues such as first aid, ventilation, lighting, and protective equipment.
- **Provincial regulations and codes:** Each province in Canada also has its own health and safety regulations, which may include additional requirements for specific industries or workplaces.

Overall, OH&S legislation and regulation in Canada are designed to protect workers from harm in the workplace, and to establish the responsibilities of employers and workers in maintaining a safe and healthy work environment.

* * *

In the USA, the Occupational Safety and Health Administration (OSHA) is the federal agency responsible for enforcing workplace safety and health regulations. OSHA sets regulations and standards that employers must follow to ensure the health and safety of their workers.

The OSHA standards cover a wide range of workplace hazards, including machinery and equipment, electrical hazards, hazardous chemicals, occupational noise exposure, and personal protective equipment.

Other relevant legislation and regulations in the USA include:

- **The Americans with Disabilities Act (ADA):** This law prohibits discrimination against people with disabilities in various areas of life, including employment. Employers must make reasonable accommodations for disabled employees.
- **The Family and Medical Leave Act (FMLA):** This law guarantees eligible employees up to 12 weeks of unpaid leave each year for certain reasons, including the birth or adoption of a child, caring for a family member with a serious health condition, or dealing with an employee's own serious health condition.
- **The Fair Labor Standards Act (FLSA):** This law sets basic minimum wage and overtime pay standards for most employees in the United States.
- **The National Institute for Occupational Safety and Health (NIOSH):** This organization conducts research on workplace health and safety issues and provides recommendations to OSHA and other agencies.

Overall, the USA has multiple laws and regulations related to occupational health and safety, with OSHA being the primary agency responsible for enforcement. Employers must adhere to these regulations to ensure the safety and well-being of their employees.

The Legal & Ethical Implications of Workplace Bullying:

Workplace bullying is a pervasive problem that can have serious legal and ethical implications. Employees who are bullied may suffer from physical and mental health problems and may also experience significant job-related stress, anxiety, and depression. Employers have a responsibility to protect their employees from bullying and harassment in the workplace, and failure to do so can result in serious legal consequences.

One of the main legal issues surrounding workplace bullying is Occupational Health and Safety (OH&S) regulations. Many countries have OH&S regulations that require employers to provide a safe and healthy work environment for their employees. Workplace bullying can be considered a hazard that poses a risk to the health and safety of employees. Employers who fail to take appropriate steps to prevent or address workplace bullying could violate these regulations and may be subject to fines or other penalties.

Another legal issue related to workplace bullying is discrimination. In many jurisdictions, employers are prohibited from discriminating against employees based on factors such as race, gender, sexual orientation, or disability. Workplace bullying motivated by discriminatory factors may be considered a form of illegal discrimination, and employers who allow or condone this behavior could face legal action.

From an ethical standpoint, workplace bullying violates basic human rights. All employees have the right to work in an environment free from abuse, harassment, and intimidation. Employers who allow or condone workplace bullying are failing to foster a culture of respect and may be contributing to a toxic work environment.

The potential consequences of workplace bullying can be significant. In addition to legal penalties, employers may face reputational damage and loss of business. Employees who are bullied may suffer from reduced productivity, absenteeism, and increased turnover. There is also a risk of employee retaliation, which can further escalate the situation and create more conflict in the workplace.

Workplace bullying is a serious issue with significant legal and ethical implications. Employers have a responsibility to provide a safe and healthy work environment for their employees and must take appropriate steps to prevent and address workplace bullying. Failure to do so can result in legal penalties, reputational damage, and damage to employee morale and productivity.

* * *

The Role Of Management In Preventing Workplace Bullying

Workplace bullying is a pervasive issue that can have a harmful impact on employees' mental and physical health, productivity, and overall well-being. Management plays a crucial role in preventing workplace bullying by fostering a culture of respect and support. In this essay, we will examine the role of management in preventing workplace bullying and discuss strategies that can create a supportive workplace culture.

Management is responsible for creating safe and healthy work environments where employees feel valued, respected, and supported. The following are strategies that can prevent workplace bullying:

1. Establish clear expectations and codes of conduct: Management should implement clear and concise policies that outline what is unacceptable behavior in the workplace. These policies should be communicated to employees, discussed regularly in team meetings, and enforced consistently.

. . .

99

2. Lead by example: Management must lead by example in showing respectful behavior in the workplace. They should model their expectations for all employees to follow.

3. Encourage open communication: Management should create an environment where employees feel comfortable reporting bullying incidents without fear of retaliation or negative consequences. They should establish open communication channels and allow for anonymous reporting of incidents.

4. Provide support and resources: Management should provide support and resources to employees subjected to workplace bullying, including counseling services, employee assistance programs, and mental health resources.

5. Invest in training and education: Management should invest in training and education programs that provide employees with the skills and knowledge needed to recognize and prevent bullying behavior in the workplace.

6. Conduct regular assessments: Management should conduct regular assessments of workplace culture and employee satisfaction to identify potential areas of improvement and address any issues that may contribute to bullying behavior in the workplace.

Management plays a crucial role in preventing workplace bullying by fostering a culture of respect and support within the organization. By putting clear policies into practice, leading by example, encouraging open communication, providing support and resources, investing in training and education, and conducting regular assessments, management can create a safe and healthy work environment where employees can thrive.

* * *

Risk Assessment, Developing & Implementing Anti-Bullying Policies And Procedures

The Importance of Risk Assessment in Preventing Workplace Bullying:

- Workplace bullying is an increasingly common issue that can negatively affect employee well-being, organizational culture, and productivity.
- Risk assessment is a critical tool for identifying the potential for bullying to occur in various workplace settings and circumstances.
- Effective risk assessment must consider a range of factors, including organizational culture, individual behaviors, and structural issues.
- The process of risk assessment enables employers to develop targeted strategies for preventing and addressing workplace bullying, such as setting clear expectations and consequences for unacceptable behavior.

- Through risk assessment, employers can also identify high-risk individuals and situations to proactively intervene and prevent future incidents of bullying.
- Effective risk assessment involves collaboration between organizational leaders, human resources professionals, and employees at all levels to gain insights into the unique challenges faced by different departments, teams, and groups.
- Investing in comprehensive, ongoing risk assessment processes can improve workplace culture, support employee well-being, and bolster corporate performance metrics, making it an essential part of addressing workplace bullying.

Risk assessment is an essential process that identifies potential hazards and risks in the workplace. It is a key aspect of preventing workplace bullying, which affects the physical and psychological well-being of employees.

By conducting a risk assessment, employers can identify the risk factors that may lead to bullying and take preventive measures to address them. Some common risk factors include poor communication, inadequate training, high workload, a lack of policies and procedures, and a toxic work environment.

A thorough risk assessment helps employers determine the likelihood and severity of bullying in the workplace. This information lets employers assess the current state of their workplace culture and create effective intervention strategies to prevent bullying from occurring.

. . .

Employers must ensure that their employees are aware of the risks of bullying and understand the steps they can take to prevent it. Through regular training on risk assessment and prevention strategies, employees can maintain a safe and healthy work environment.

Risk assessment is a critical part of preventing workplace bullying. By identifying potential risk factors, employees and employers can work together to create a positive and healthy workplace culture that promotes respect, dignity, and professionalism.

* * *

Developing An Oh&S Plan For Workplace Bullying Prevention

A Framework for Developing a Comprehensive OH&S Plan for Preventing Workplace Bullying:

- **Recognize the Impact of Workplace Bullying on Your Organization:** Highlight the effects of workplace bullying on company culture, employee morale, productivity, and the bottom line.

- **Identify the Key Elements of an Effective OH&S Plan for Workplace Bullying Prevention:** Discuss the essential parts of an OH&S plan, such as establishing a policy against bullying, providing training, setting up a reporting mechanism, and taking corrective actions.

- **Conduct a Risk Assessment:** Outline strategies for identifying and assessing the risk of workplace bullying in your organization. Discuss how to survey employees, analyze incident reports, investigate complaints, and gather other relevant data.

- **Establish Policies and Procedures:** Explain how to create clear and concise policies and procedures against bullying that align with your organization's culture and values. Discuss the importance of communicating these policies clearly and enforcing them consistently.
- **Provide Training and Awareness Programs:** Discuss strategies for providing training and awareness programs to employees, managers, and supervisors. Emphasize the importance of educating all stakeholders, including bystanders, about the negative impacts of bullying and how to intervene.
- **Establish a Reporting Mechanism:** Highlight the importance of providing employees with a safe and confidential reporting mechanism for complaints related to workplace bullying. Discuss how to establish a system for receiving, investigating, and resolving complaints.
- **Monitor and Evaluate Your OH&S Plan:** Provide guidance on how to monitor and evaluate the effectiveness of your OH&S plan for preventing workplace bullying. Emphasize the need for ongoing measurement and feedback to ensure continuous improvement.

Developing A Comprehensive OH&S Plan for Preventing Workplace Bullying:

Workplace bullying can harm both the employee and the overall productivity of an organization. So it is essential to develop a comprehensive Occupational Health and Safety (OH&S) plan to prevent workplace bullying from happening. The following framework provides a step-by-step guide for developing such a plan:

. . .

Step 1: Establish a Bullying Policy

The first step in preventing workplace bullying is to establish a bullying policy. This policy should outline what constitutes bullying in the workplace and what the consequences will be for engaging in such behavior. It should also provide clear instructions on how employees can report bullying incidents and what steps will be taken to address them.

Step 2: Train Employees and Managers

It is essential to train both employees and managers on workplace bullying. Employees need to know what constitutes bullying and how to report it. Managers need to know how to identify and address bullying incidents and how to support employees who report this behavior.

Step 3: Create a Reporting System

Create a system that lets employees report bullying incidents anonymously if they wish. Make sure employees know how to use the system, and that there are clear procedures for handling reports. Ensure that the system is accessible and easy to use.

Step 4: Investigate Complaints

Investigate all bullying complaints promptly and impartially. Make sure the person responsible for investigating the report has the training and expertise to handle the case. Interview all parties involved and gather any evidence that may relate to the case.

Step 5: Take Action

Take appropriate action against the alleged bully if the investigation confirms the incident. The consequences should follow the company's bullying policy, and any required sanctions should be clearly communicated to the affected parties. Support the victim by providing counseling, training or any necessary assistance.

Step 6: Monitor and Review the Plan

Monitor the effectiveness of the bullying prevention plan regularly. Collect feedback from employees and assess the number of reported incidents. Review and update the plan based on the lessons learned.

Preventing workplace bullying requires a comprehensive OH&S plan that involves creating a policy, training employees and managers, creating a reporting system, investigating complaints, taking appropriate action and reviewing the plan regularly. By following the above framework, organizations can create a safe and harmonious workplace where employees feel valued and respected.

The Importance of Monitoring & Evaluating the Effectiveness of Workplace Bullying Prevention Strategies:

Workplace bullying can have a serious impact on the health and well-being of employees, leading to physical and mental health problems, decreased job satisfaction, lower productivity, and even a high turnover rate. So organizations must take proactive steps to prevent and address workplace bullying.

One strategy that organizations can use to prevent bullying is to develop and implement workplace bullying prevention strategies. Introducing policies, training programs, complaint procedures, and supportive workplace culture are some measures that can be taken to prevent workplace bullying. However, it is essential to monitor and evaluate the effectiveness of these strategies to make sure they are yielding the desired results.

Monitoring and evaluating the effectiveness of workplace

bullying prevention strategies is vital for various reasons. First, it enables organizations to track their progress and determine whether they are making headway toward reducing or preventing workplace bullying. With regular monitoring and evaluation, organizations can identify what is working and what is not, make necessary changes, and improve upon existing efforts.

Second, monitoring and evaluating the effectiveness of workplace bullying prevention strategies helps to assess the impact of these strategies on employees' morale, health, productivity, and other workplace-related outcomes. Continuous evaluation lets organizations determine whether they are providing a safe and healthy working environment and how well they are meeting their legal and ethical obligations.

Finally, monitoring and evaluating the effectiveness of workplace bullying prevention strategies promotes transparency and accountability. Organizations that regularly monitor and evaluate their strategies can show their commitment to taking workplace bullying seriously and to safeguarding their employees' well-being.

Monitoring and evaluating the effectiveness of workplace bullying prevention strategies are crucial for organizations that want to create a safe and healthy working environment for their employees. The continuous evaluation process lets organizations assess the progress made in preventing bullying, identify challenges and opportunities for improvement, and ensure transparency and accountability. By investing in monitoring and evaluating workplace bullying prevention strategies, organizations can reduce the prevalence of bullying and promote a more positive workplace culture.

* * *

Case Studies And Best Practices For Workplace Bullying Prevention

Case Study 1: The University of Michigan's Workplace Bullying Prevention & Response Policy

Introduction to the University of Michigan and its commitment to preventing and addressing workplace bullying:

The University of Michigan is a renowned educational institution committed to providing a positive and inclusive working environment for all its staff, students, and faculty. One of the core values of the university is to create a culture of respect, dignity, and equity.

The university implemented a comprehensive Workplace Bullying Prevention and Response Policy in 2015. The policy includes a range of preventive measures, including education and training for employees, clear reporting procedures, and disciplinary actions for employees who engage in bullying behavior.

. . .

To ensure the policy's effectiveness, the university created a Bullying Prevention and Response Committee that meets regularly to review policy implementation and make recommendations for improvement. The committee also reviews reports of bullying and provides support to both victims and perpetrators.

To uphold this commitment, the university has put in place extensive policies and guidelines that aim to prevent and address all forms of workplace bullying. The university recognizes that bullying is a serious issue that can have severe mental, emotional, and physical repercussions on its employees.

The university has made it clear that all forms of bullying and harassment will not be tolerated, and strict disciplinary actions will be taken against any perpetrators. The institution has created safe channels for reporting any incidents of bullying, and the university administration ensures these reports are dealt with swiftly and sensitively.

The university takes great pride in providing a safe and inclusive working environment for all its employees, and it strives to provide them with the support and resources to address any issues that may arise. The institution remains committed to fostering a culture of respect and unity, where everyone can thrive and grow without fear of intimidation or discrimination.

Description of the development and implementation of the University's Workplace Bullying Prevention and Response Policy:

The University of Michigan has taken an important step toward providing a safe and inclusive workplace for all employees with the development and implementation of their Workplace Bullying Prevention and Response Policy. The goal of this policy is to uphold the University's commitment to providing a respectful and professional work environment, free from any form of bullying, harassment or discrimination.

The policy is broad and covers all employees, including faculty, staff, student employees, temporary employees, and volunteers. The policy defines workplace bullying as repeated aggressive or intimidating behavior, whether verbal or physical, that is intended to harm, humiliate or undermine an individual or group.

The Policy outlines a clear set of procedures for reporting, responding to and addressing incidents of workplace bullying. These procedures include reporting incidents to a designated individual or office, investigation and resolution of complaints, and supportive measures for employees who have experienced bullying.

In addition to responding to incidents of bullying, the policy also includes a focus on prevention strategies, including training and education for employees on recognizing and preventing workplace bullying.

Overall, the University's Workplace Bullying Prevention and Response Policy shows a commitment to fostering a safe and respectful workplace culture, where all employees can feel valued, supported and able to work to their full potential.

. . .

The University of Michigan's Analysis of the effectiveness of the policy:

The University of Michigan's policy on addressing and preventing sexual misconduct, harassment, and discrimination has been in effect since its implementation. Since then, the effectiveness of the policy has been evaluated often to make sure it follows current laws, regulations, and best practices. This analysis considers the feedback provided by staff, managers, and other stakeholders and the data on reports, investigations, and outcomes.

Overall, the University's policy has been effective in addressing and preventing sexual misconduct, harassment, and discrimination. The policy makes sure all reports of such incidents are taken seriously and investigated thoroughly. The University has seen an increase in the number of reports of sexual misconduct, harassment, and discrimination in recent years, which suggests that the policy is encouraging individuals to come forward and report incidents.

Managers and supervisors are also regularly trained on the policy, which helps them to identify and prevent issues in the workplace. The University has also put preventative measures into practice, such as educational campaigns and training programs for students and employees that emphasize the importance of respect and consent. These initiatives have been well-received by staff and students, who acknowledge the value of these programs in promoting a more inclusive and respectful culture on campus.

Data on reports, investigations, and outcomes further support the effectiveness of the University's policy. The University has seen an increase in the number of investigations into incidents of sexual misconduct, harassment, and discrimination, which suggests that the policy is being used by individuals to hold those who engage in this behavior accountable. Additionally, the University has seen an increase in the number of individuals sanctioned for engaging in sexual misconduct, harassment, and discrimination, which indicates that the policy is effective in deterring this behavior and making sure appropriate consequences are enforced.

Based on the feedback from staff, managers, and other stakeholders and data on reports, investigations, and outcomes, the University of Michigan's policy on addressing and preventing sexual misconduct, harassment, and discrimination has been found to be effective. The policy ensures that reports of such incidents are taken seriously, investigated thoroughly, and individuals engaging in such behavior are held accountable. The University's preventative measures, such as educational campaigns and training programs, have also been effective in promoting a more respectful and inclusive culture on campus.

Discussion of challenges and opportunities found during the policy's implementation:

The implementation of the University of Michigan's new policy has not been without its challenges and opportunities. One of the major issues faced during its implementation has been resistance from some employees who do not fully agree with the policy. This has resulted in a lack of cooperation and understanding and delays in the enforcement of the policy.

Confidentiality concerns have also been a significant obstacle during the policy's implementation. This has led to some employees withholding important information or reporting violations to avoid possible breaches of confidentiality. As a result, it has become increasingly important for the university to develop new methods of reporting and handling confidential information in a safe and secure manner.

Training needs have emerged as another challenge during the implementation process. With the introduction of new policies and guidelines, employees require extensive training and education to ensure they fully understand what is expected of them. This includes sensitive topics such as discrimination, harassment, and other forms of unacceptable behavior. So, it is crucial to provide regular training and updates to ensure all employees are properly equipped to understand and follow the new policy.

Overall, the challenges and opportunities found during the implementation of the policy have highlighted the need for communication, transparency, and support from all parties involved. Addressing these issues head-on will ensure the University of Michigan creates an environment welcoming, respectful, inclusive, and safe for all members of its community.

Comparison With Other Workplace Bullying Policies and Practices:

The University of Michigan's workplace bullying policy is similar to other policies because it defines workplace bullying as repeated negative behavior intended to harm, intimidate, or undermine the victim. It also includes examples of prohibited conduct, such as verbal abuse, exclusion, and interference with work performance.

. . .

One difference is that the University of Michigan's policy specifically addresses cyberbullying and social media harassment. It also requires managers and supervisors to take proactive steps to prevent workplace bullying and to respond promptly and appropriately to complaints.

In terms of best practices, the University of Michigan's policy emphasizes the importance of creating a safe and respectful workplace culture where employees feel comfortable reporting bullying behavior. It also provides resources for employees who experience or witness workplace bullying, such as confidential counseling services and an employee assistance program.

Overall, the University of Michigan's workplace bullying policy serves as a strong example of a comprehensive and proactive approach to preventing and addressing workplace bullying.

Lessons learned and recommendations for improving the policy and promoting a respectful work culture at the University and beyond:

The University of Michigan has been in the news recently due to several allegations of sexual misconduct and harassment among faculty and staff. These incidents have highlighted the need for stronger policies and a more respectful work culture at the University and beyond.

Lessons learned from these incidents include the importance of clear policies and procedures for reporting incidents of misconduct, a more proactive approach to prevention and education, and a respectful workplace culture that values and respects all employees.

To improve the policy and promote a respectful work culture, the University must take several steps. This includes:

1. Strengthen the policy: The University must review their current policy on sexual misconduct and harassment, and make necessary revisions to ensure it is comprehensive, consistent, and easily understood. Additionally, they must provide regular training for all employees on the policy, reporting procedures, and prevention strategies.

2. Increase accountability: The University must hold those who violate the policy accountable for their actions. This includes taking prompt action when incidents are reported, conducting timely investigations, and imposing consequences for those found responsible.

3. Improve prevention efforts: The University must implement a comprehensive prevention program that includes education and training for all employees, bystander intervention strategies, and ongoing communication about the importance of creating a respectful work environment.

4. Foster a respectful work culture: The University must create a work environment that values diversity, equity, and inclusion, and promotes respect and civility among all employees. This can be achieved through leadership commitment, effective communication, and ongoing professional development.

The University of Michigan has a responsibility to ensure that all
employees can work in a safe, respectful, and inclusive environment.
By taking the necessary steps to strengthen their policies, increase
accountability, improve prevention efforts, and foster a respectful
work culture, the University can show their commitment to creating a
workplace where everyone can thrive.

Case Study 2: The Bank of Ireland's Zero Tolerance of Workplace Bullying Policy

Background and context of the Bank of Ireland's zero tolerance of workplace bullying policy:

The Bank of Ireland is one of the oldest and most respected financial
institutions in Ireland, with roots dating back to 1783. Over the years,
the bank has built a reputation for delivering high-quality financial
services to customers across Ireland and the UK.

In recent years, the Bank of Ireland has recognized the growing
problem of workplace bullying within the organization and in 2017
created a policy addressing all forms of bullying, including cyberbullying, and outlines clear reporting procedures and disciplinary
actions for employees who violate the policy.

In addition to the policy, the Bank created a Bullying and Harassment Support and Reporting Line that provides employees with
confidential support and guidance on how to handle workplace
bullying situations. The bank also provides training sessions for
employees and managers on how to prevent and respond to bullying
in the workplace.

. . .

Because of the policy and support systems, the Bank of Ireland has seen an improvement in employee morale and a reduction in stress-related absences. Additionally, the bank was recognized with an award for excellence in healthcare and well-being by the Irish Heart Foundation due to its commitment to creating a healthy and positive work environment.

The Bank has taken a proactive approach to addressing workplace bullying by implementing a zero-tolerance policy. This policy sets out clear guidelines for what constitutes workplace bullying, including both overt and subtle behaviors.

The policy also outlines the consequences of engaging in workplace bullying, which can include disciplinary action, termination of employment, or legal action if the behavior is a criminal offense.

The Bank's zero-tolerance policy is in line with the organization's core values, which emphasize respect and fairness for all employees. By taking a firm stance on workplace bullying, the Bank of Ireland is sending a clear message that this behavior will not be tolerated, and employees can expect to be held accountable for their actions.

Overall, the Bank of Ireland's zero tolerance of workplace bullying policy reflects the organization's commitment to creating a positive and inclusive workplace culture. Through this policy, the bank aims to make sure all employees feel safe, respected, and valued, which ultimately contributes to the overall success of the organization.

· · ·

The Development and Implementation of the Policy:

The Bank of Ireland has a strong commitment to corporate social responsibility and has recognized the importance of developing and putting policies into practice that reflect this commitment. One such policy is the sustainable lending policy, which outlines the bank's commitment to promoting sustainable development through its lending practices.

The development of the sustainable lending policy involved consultation with a range of internal and external stakeholders, including employees, customers, regulators, NGOs and industry bodies. The bank recognized that to create a policy that would be effective and sustainable, it was important to engage with these stakeholders to understand their views and concerns.

Internal consultation involved engagement with employees across the bank through a range of channels, including workshops, focus groups and surveys. These discussions provided valuable feedback and insights into how the policy could be developed and implemented in a way that was practical and effective.

External consultation involved engagement with a range of stakeholders, including customers, regulators, NGOs and industry bodies. The bank worked closely with these stakeholders to understand their views on sustainable lending, and to make sure the policy reflected best practice in the industry.

Once the policy had been developed, it was communicated to all employees across the bank through a range of channels, including training sessions, intranet updates and staff briefings. The bank also engaged with customers and external stakeholders to ensure that they were aware of the policy and its implications.

Overall, the development and implementation of the sustainable lending policy was a collaborative process that involved consultation with a range of internal and external stakeholders. The bank recognized that to be effective, the policy needed to reflect the concerns and aspirations of all stakeholders, and that engagement was essential to achieving this. By listening to and engaging with its employees and external stakeholders, the bank has developed a policy that reflects its commitment to corporate social responsibility and sustainable development.

Impact of the Policy on the Organization:
The Bank of Ireland's policy changes have had a significant impact on the organization, including changes in employee behaviors and perceptions. The policy changes have led to improvements in the bank's risk management practices and its overall financial stability. However, the changes have also brought about challenges for employees to adapt to new processes and policies.

Implementing the policy changes required employees to undergo training and become more cautious in their decision-making processes. This has led to a more careful and accountable workforce, which has helped to reduce risk and losses. The changes have also led to a greater emphasis on customer service, with employees spending more time listening to customer concerns and offering solutions.

. . .

Despite the benefits, the policy changes have also resulted in some negative employee perceptions. For example, the emphasis on compliance has led some employees to feel they are being micromanaged and unable to use their own judgment. Moreover, implementing the policy has been met with resistance from some employees who fear the changes will be damaging for the bank and their own careers.

The Bank of Ireland's policy changes have had a significant impact on the organization, including changes in employee behaviors and perceptions. The changes have led to improvements in risk management practices, customer service, and financial stability. However, they have also posed challenges relating to employee adaptation and perception. Overall, the bank must continue to evaluate the impact of its policy changes to ensure the organization can balance customer service, risk management, and employee satisfaction.

Challenges and barriers faced in putting the policy into practice and how they were addressed:

As one of the leading banks in Ireland, the Bank of Ireland has always been at the forefront of implementing policies that benefit its customers and employees. However, implementing these policies often poses several challenges and barriers that require careful consideration and planning.

One of the most significant challenges faced by the Bank of Ireland in putting policies into practice is resistance from stakeholders. This may include employees resistant to change or customers accustomed to the way things have always been done. To address this challenge, the bank has focused on effective communication and engagement with stakeholders. The bank has made a concerted effort to explain the reasoning behind the policy and how it will help all stakeholders.

Another challenge faced by the Bank of Ireland is the complexity of its operations. As a large and diverse organization, putting policies into practice may require significant changes to existing processes and procedures. The bank has tackled this challenge by breaking down the policy into clear and actionable steps that can be started in stages. This approach makes sure the policy is put into practice successfully without disrupting business operations.

Finally, the Bank of Ireland faces external barriers that can hinder policy implementation. These may include changes in the economic and regulatory environment or unexpected events such as pandemics. To address these challenges, the bank engages in continuous monitoring and evaluation of its policies, making sure they remain relevant and effective in a rapidly changing environment.

The Bank of Ireland faces several challenges and barriers in putting policies into practice. However, through effective communication and engagement with stakeholders, breaking down complex policies into clear and actionable steps, and continuous monitoring and evaluation, the bank has succeeded in implementing policies that benefit its customers and employees.

The role of leadership in enforcing the policy and creating a culture of respect and accountability:

The Bank of Ireland is a leading institution responsible for providing financial services to the people of Ireland. Leadership plays a crucial role in enforcing policies and creating a culture of respect and accountability within the bank.

The leadership of the Bank of Ireland must lead by example and show their commitment to the values and principles of the organization. They should make sure all employees understand and adhere to the policies, particularly those that relate to respect and ethical behavior.

The bank's leaders should also take an active role in creating a positive culture within the organization. They should encourage open communication and feedback, and make sure every employee feels valued, respected, and supported.

Leadership must enforce policies through training and education. They should provide regular training to all employees, particularly those in management positions, to help them understand the policies and their importance. This will ensure that all employees are aware of their responsibilities, and the consequences of not adhering to the policy.

The leadership should create an accountability mechanism within the bank. Employees must be held accountable for their actions, particularly when it comes to adhering to the policies of the bank. This should include regular assessments of employee performance, including their adherence to bank policies.

. . .

Strong leadership is essential for enforcing policies and creating a culture of respect and accountability within the Bank of Ireland. By showing their commitment to these values and investing in training and education, the leaders of the bank can create a positive culture that empowers employees to act with integrity and provide excellent service to customers.

Evaluation & Monitoring of the Policy's Effectiveness:

As a financial institution, the Bank of Ireland recognizes the importance of evaluating and monitoring the effectiveness of its policies. The bank has established a robust system to assess the impact of its policies, including feedback mechanisms and ongoing training.

The Bank of Ireland regularly review policies to ensure they remain effective and up-to-date with current industry practices and regulations. This includes conducting ongoing assessments of the policy's efficiency and determining the areas that need improvement. The bank also considers the views of customers, employees, and stakeholders in determining the policies' effectiveness.

To effectively monitor and evaluate policies, the Bank of Ireland has established feedback mechanisms that let customers provide feedback and submit complaints if they feel unsatisfied with the policies in place. The bank also actively encourages its employees to provide feedback on the policies' effectiveness, which enables it to address any concerns promptly. This feedback helps in identifying challenges and taking corrective measures where necessary.

The Bank of Ireland recognizes that the financial industry is continuously changing, and ongoing training is essential in ensuring employees are up to date with the latest industry trends and regulations. The bank provides employees with regular training programs to enhance their skills and knowledge on the policies in place. It also makes sure all employees undergo compliance training to ensure they adhere to the set policies and regulations.

The Bank of Ireland's commitment to evaluating and monitoring the effectiveness of its policies makes sure it remains relevant and responsive to the needs of its customers, employees, and stakeholders. The provision of feedback mechanisms and ongoing training programs are essential parts of ensuring the bank's policies are effective in meeting its set goals.

Lessons learned from the Bank of Ireland's experience that could be applied to other organizations seeking to address workplace bullying:

The Bank of Ireland's experience revealed several lessons that can be applied to other organizations seeking to address workplace bullying. These include:

1. Taking a proactive approach: The bank's leadership took a proactive approach to address workplace bullying by developing policies and procedures to prevent and respond to incidents of bullying.

2. Encouraging open communication: The bank fostered a culture of open communication where employees were encouraged to speak up about instances of bullying, and managers were trained to listen and respond appropriately.

. . .

3. Providing training: The bank invested in training for its employees and managers on identifying and addressing workplace bullying. This training helped to increase awareness and equipped employees with the skills needed to handle bullying incidents.

4. Holding individuals accountable: The bank held individuals accountable for their actions, and sanctions were imposed on those found to have engaged in bullying behavior.

5. Providing support for victims: The bank provided support for victims of workplace bullying, including counseling services and access to employee assistance programs.

6. Continuously monitoring and reviewing: The bank's leadership continuously monitored and reviewed its policies and procedures to make sure they remained effective in addressing workplace bullying.

7. Striving for a positive workplace culture: The bank's leadership consistently promoted a positive and respectful workplace culture and encouraged employees to work collaboratively toward meeting the bank's goals.

Overall, the Bank of Ireland's experience highlights the importance of taking a proactive approach to address workplace bullying, fostering open communication, providing training, holding individuals accountable, providing support for victims, continuously monitoring and reviewing policies and procedures, and striving for a positive workplace culture. These lessons can be applied to other organizations seeking to address workplace bullying and create a safe and healthy work environment.

Case Study 3: The Australian Human Rights Commission's Workplace Discrimination & Harassment Prevention Program

Overview of the Australian Human Rights Commission's Workplace Discrimination and Harassment Prevention Program:

The Australian Human Rights Commission's Workplace Discrimination and Harassment Prevention Program is a comprehensive initiative aimed at preventing and addressing discrimination and harassment in Australian workplaces. The program is designed to provide practical guidance and support to employers, employees, and managers to promote a respectful and inclusive workplace culture.

The Commission created its Workplace Discrimination and Harassment Prevention Program in 1984. The program has continued to evolve since then to include specific measures for preventing and responding to workplace bullying.

The program offers a range of services, including training and education programs, advisory services, and resources to help employers develop effective policies and procedures. It also assists employees who have experienced discrimination or harassment in the workplace, offering advice and support to help them protect their legal rights. As well it provides mediation and conciliation services to resolve bullying complaints.

. . .

The program has a strong focus on promoting diversity and inclusion and encourages employers to embrace practices that promote a diverse and inclusive workplace culture. It also provides guidance on how to address unconscious bias and promote respectful communication in the workplace.

The Australian Human Rights Commission's Workplace Discrimination and Harassment Prevention Program is an important initiative that plays a crucial role in creating a more inclusive and respectful workplace environment in Australia. By providing education and support to employers and employees, the program is helping to improve workplace practices and promote a culture of fairness and equality for all.

Importance of Addressing Workplace Discrimination & Harassment:

The Australian Human Rights Commission's Workplace Discrimination and Harassment Prevention Program was designed to promote and protect human rights by providing guidelines and training to prevent discrimination and harassment in the workplace. Workplace discrimination and harassment can cause significant harm to individuals, affecting their mental and physical health, productivity, and job performance.

Denying someone equal employment opportunities or making them feel uncomfortable or unsafe in the workplace can have long-lasting effects on their career and can affect their ability to gain promotions or access further employment opportunities. Workplace harassment can lead to employees leaving their jobs, ultimately costing the organization both money and human resources.

It is important to address and prevent workplace discrimination and harassment, not only to protect the rights and well-being of individual employees, but also to ensure a healthy, productive and inclusive work environment that benefits the organization. By promoting diversity and inclusivity, organizations can increase their talent pool and create a welcoming, safe and supportive environment that cultivates talent and promotes collaboration and innovation, ultimately leading to greater performance and success.

Methodology of the Program:

The Australian Human Rights Commission's Workplace Discrimination and Harassment Prevention Program is a comprehensive approach designed to help businesses and organizations create and foster safer, more inclusive workplace cultures. The program takes a systematic and evidence-based approach, using a variety of methodologies to gather insights and feedback from both employers and employees.

One of the key parts of the program is a series of surveys designed to gather data on workplace culture, diversity and inclusion, and incidents of discrimination and harassment. The surveys are anonymous, voluntary, and tailored to specific industries and organizational contexts, letting the Commission gather rich data about the experiences of employees across a variety of workplaces.

. . .

In addition to the survey part, the program involves in-depth consultation with key stakeholders, including employers, employee representatives, industry associations, and other experts. Through interviews, focus groups, and other methods, the Commission seeks to engage with a broad range of perspectives and experiences, identify best practices, and develop tailored solutions to address workplace discrimination and harassment.

Overall, the method of the program is designed to be inclusive, collaborative, and grounded in sound research and evidence. By engaging with employers and employees in a variety of ways, the Commission can offer valuable insights and support to help organizations in creating more equitable and respectful workplace environments.

Implementation and results of the program in workplaces across Australia:

The Australian Human Rights Commission's Workplace Discrimination and Harassment Prevention Program is an initiative aimed at creating safe and respectful workplaces across Australia. The program provides tools and resources to help employers in preventing and addressing discrimination and harassment in the workplace.

Implementing the program has been met with positive results, with many workplaces across the country adopting the program's strategies and reporting significant improvements in workplace culture. The program's approach focuses on prevention rather than reactive measures, encouraging employers to put preventative measures into practice such as workplace policies, training programs, and reporting mechanisms to create a more inclusive and respectful workplace environment.

Because of the program's implementation, workplaces have reported a decrease in the occurrence of workplace discrimination and harassment. This has resulted in improved employee engagement, productivity, and retention rates. Employers who have implemented the program have also reported a positive impact on their organization's reputation, with many citing an increase in customer loyalty and satisfaction.

The Australian Human Rights Commission's Workplace Discrimination and Harassment Prevention Program has proven to be an effective tool for employers in creating safe and inclusive workplaces. By working toward prevention and putting proactive measures into practice, workplaces can create a culture of respect and inclusion that benefits both employees and the organizations they work in.

Success Stories and Challenges Faced During Implementation:

The Australian Human Rights Commission's Workplace Discrimination and Harassment Prevention Program (WDHPP) is an initiative aimed at promoting respect and dignity in the workplace by preventing discrimination and harassment based on gender, race, age, disability, and other grounds. Since its launch, the program has recorded successes and challenges during implementation.

Success stories of the WDHPP include the testimonies of employees who have benefited from the program. For example, some employees have reported feeling more confident and secure in their workplace because of the training offered by the program. Others have stated that the program has helped them to better understand their rights and responsibilities as employees, and how to exercise them effectively. Additionally, some organizations have reported a reduction in the incidence of discrimination and harassment following the implementation of the WDHPP.

However, implementing the WDHPP has also presented challenges. One of such challenges is the resistance faced from some organizations, who view the program as a burden or an intrusion into their autonomy. Some organizations have also expressed concerns about the cost and time investment required to implement the program successfully. Additionally, there has been a lack of awareness among some employees about the program or its relevance to their work.

The Australian Human Rights Commission's WDHPP has recorded successes and challenges during implementation. The program's successes, including the testimonies of employees, reflect the important role that such initiatives can play in promoting respectful and harmonious workplaces. However, the challenges encountered suggest the need for continued dialogue and education with employers and employees to create long-lasting change.

Analysis of the impact of the program on workplace culture and reduction of discrimination & harassment incidents:

The Australian Human Rights Commission's WDHPP has had a significant impact on workplace culture, resulting in a reduction of discrimination and harassment incidents. The program has helped to raise awareness about the negative impact of discrimination and harassment on individuals and the workplace environment. It has encouraged workplaces to create a culture of respect and inclusion, where everyone is valued and treated with dignity.

Through the program, workplaces have been able to identify and address areas of discrimination and harassment, resulting in a reduction of incidents. Measures such as developing policies and procedures for reporting and addressing discrimination and harassment, providing training for employees, and empowering staff to respond to incidents have all contributed to this reduction. The program has also helped workplaces to create a safe and supportive environment for employees to report incidents, without fear of retaliation.

The impact of the program has extended beyond the workplace, with many workplaces using the knowledge and skills gained through the program to promote inclusion and respect in their communities. The program has helped to shift attitudes toward discrimination and harassment, resulting in a greater willingness to speak out against these behaviors.

Overall, the Australian Human Rights Commission's WDHPP has helped to promote respect and inclusion in workplaces, resulting in a reduction of discrimination and harassment incidents. It has created a culture of respect and dignity, which has extended beyond the workplace, creating a more inclusive society.

. . .

Recommendations for employers and policymakers to adopt similar programs for preventing workplace discrimination & harassment:

1. Develop policies and procedures aimed at preventing workplace discrimination and harassment. These policies should clearly define what constitutes discrimination and harassment, outline the process for making complaints, and provide remedies for victims.

2. Train managers and employees in the policies and procedures, as well as on the importance of preventing discrimination and harassment in the workplace.

3. Develop reporting systems that allow employees to make complaints in a safe and confidential manner.

4. Investigate complaints in a timely and thorough manner and impose sanctions on those found to have engaged in discrimination or harassment.

5. Develop strategies for preventing discrimination and harassment, such as promoting diversity and inclusion, and creating workplace cultures that value respect and dignity for all employees.

6. Regularly review and evaluate the effectiveness of the prevention program to identify areas for improvement.

. . .

7. Finally, employers and policymakers should focus on the prevention of workplace discrimination and harassment by supporting ongoing education and training opportunities, as well as by creating regulatory frameworks that ensure compliance with relevant laws and regulations.

Because of the program, the Australian Human Rights Commission has seen a reduction in reports of workplace bullying and an improvement in employee morale. The program has also helped establish clear expectations for behavior in the workplace and a culture of respect and inclusivity.

Here Are A Few Examples of Workplace Bullying Prevention & Intervention Strategies Used by Organizations:

The Healthy Workplace Bill: The Healthy Workplace Bill is a proposed piece of legislation introduced in several U.S. states. The bill would make workplace bullying illegal and would give employees the right to take legal action against their bullies.

Workplace Bullying Prevention and Intervention Policy: Many organizations have put policies into practice that clearly define what constitutes workplace bullying and provide employees with a clear process for reporting incidents of bullying. These policies also outline the steps that the organization will take to investigate and address reports of bullying.

Employee Training and Education: Organizations can provide training and education to their employees on how to recognize and prevent workplace bullying. This training can include topics such as communication skills, conflict resolution, and emotional intelligence.

Employee Support: Organizations can provide employees with support resources such as counseling services, employee assistance programs, and peer support groups. These resources can help employees who have been bullied to cope with the emotional effects of the bullying and can also help to prevent future incidents of bullying.

Employee Feedback Mechanisms: Organizations can implement employee feedback mechanisms such as employee surveys or suggestion boxes to let employees provide feedback on their workplace environment. This feedback can identify potential bullying incidents and to make changes to prevent future incidents from occurring.

Overall, preventing and addressing workplace bullying requires a comprehensive approach that includes policies, training, education, support, and feedback mechanisms. By implementing these strategies, organizations can create a safe and healthy workplace environment for all employees.

Best Practices for Workplace Bullying Prevention:

Bullying is a serious concern within the workplace, often leading to decreased productivity, low morale, and even legal issues. Employers must take preventive measures to create a safe and healthy work environment for their employees. Here are some best practices for workplace bullying prevention and success stories from different industries and organizations.

. . .

1. Develop a Clear Anti-Bullying Policy: An effective bullying prevention program should have a comprehensive policy in place that explains what constitutes bullying, how to report the incident, the steps involved in investigation, and the disciplinary measures for offenders. It is essential to communicate this policy to all employees, make it easily accessible and enforce it consistently.

Success Story: Walmart introduced a strict policy against bullying and harassment, which led to a reduction in the number of complaints and increased employee engagement and satisfaction.

2. Encourage Open Communication: Encourage communication among employees to create an inclusive work culture. Encourage employees to report any incidents of bullying or harassment without fear of retaliation. Train employees in how to handle conflicts and provide them with the necessary resources to resolve conflicts before they escalate.

Success Story: Google has a workplace culture that promotes open communication and transparency. They encourage regular feedback and provide channels for employees to report any incidents of bullying or harassment anonymously.

3. Provide Training and Education: Provide regular training and education to employees to educate them about bullying and its negative consequences, how to recognize it, prevent it, and handle the situation. The training should be aimed at sensitizing employees and supervisors about the effects of bullying, the importance of a respectful and supportive work environment, and how to resolve conflicts.

Success Story: L'Oreal Paris introduced a mandatory training program for all its employees to raise awareness of workplace bullying and harassment, which has significantly reduced incidents of bad behavior between staff members.

4. Foster a Culture of Respect and Civility: Work on creating a workplace culture that promotes respect, civility, and professionalism at all levels. Lead by example and hold everyone accountable for their behavior.

Success Story: U.S. Navy implemented a "Culture of Excellence" initiative, which emphasized respect and accountability. This program focused on empowering individuals to promote professional behavior and held those who treated others poorly accountable.

5. Follow Through with Consequences: It is essential to follow through on the consequences for bullying, as set out in company policies. Any action that goes against the anti-bullying policy should result in disciplinary action, including termination.

Success Story: Kaiser Permanente implemented policies that provided disciplinary action for those who participated in bullying or harassment. This led to a decrease in incidents of workplace bullying and increased job satisfaction.

.   .   .

Creating a positive and respectful work environment is essential in preventing workplace bullying. It is the responsibility of leaders and management to encourage open communication, provide training, and follow through on protecting their employees. Implementing these best practices will create a healthier and safer work environment where employees can thrive personally and professionally.

* * *

Conclusion

As I have retired from the workforce, I am unlikely to encounter a bully at work. But as a writer and self-publisher in my own business, the possibility is there with my clients and people I encounter in the public.

Bullies are everywhere. I'm hopeful that by reading this book you are more knowledgeable and self-confident in dealing with bullies you encounter or perhaps helping another in need.

Life is a lot more enjoyable when you need not worry that a bully has you in their sights.

Take care!

Rae A. Stonehouse

Additional Resources:

Note that this is not an exhaustive list and there may be other valuable resources available in these regions.

North America:

Occupational Safety and Health Administration (OSHA): https://www.osha.gov/

Canadian Centre for Occupational Health and Safety (CCOHS): https://www.ccohs.ca/

National Institute for Occupational Safety and Health (NIOSH): https://www.cdc.gov/niosh/index.htm

Great Britain:

Health and Safety Executive (HSE): https://www.hse.gov.uk/

Institution of Occupational Safety and Health (IOSH): https://www.iosh.com/

New Zealand/Australia:

WorkSafe New Zealand: https://worksafe.govt.nz/

SafeWork Australia: https://www.safeworkaustralia.gov.au/

About the Author

Rae A. Stonehouse is a Canadian born author & speaker. His professional career as a Registered Nurse working predominantly in psychiatry/mental health, has spanned four decades.

Rae has embraced the principal of CANI (Constant and Never-ending Improvement) as promoted by thought leaders such as Tony Robbins and brings that philosophy to each of his publications and presentations.

Rae has dedicated the latter segment of his journey through life to overcoming his personal
inhibitions. As a 29+ year member of Toastmasters International he has systematically built his self-confidence and communicating ability.

He is passionate about sharing his lessons with his readers and listeners.

His publications thus far are of the self-help, self-improvement genre and systematically offer valuable sage advice on a specific topic.

His writing style can be described as being conversational. As an author Rae strives to have a one-to-one conversation with each of his readers, very much like having your own personal self-development coach.

Rae is known for having a wry sense of humor that features in his publications. To learn more about Rae A. Stonehouse, **visit The Wonderful World of Rae Stonehouse** at https://raestonehouse.com

Facebook: https://www.facebook.com/raestonehouse.aws
Twitter: https://twitter.com/raestonehouse

* * *

Also, By Rae A. Stonehouse

Visit https://liveforexcellence.store/ for a selection of personal/professional self-development books by Rae A. Stonehouse.

If you have found this book to be helpful, please leave us a warm review wherever you purchased it.

* * *

www.ingramcontent.com/pod-product-compliance
Lightning Source LLC
Chambersburg PA
CBHW050508210326
41521CB00011B/2374